Love: A Fruit Always in Season

Love

A Fruit Always in Season

Daily Meditations
From the Words of

MOTHER TERESA OF CALCUTTA

Selected and Edited by
DOROTHY S. HUNT

IGNATIUS PRESS   SAN FRANCISCO

Cover photograph by Michael Collopy
Cover design by Marcia Ryan

With ecclesiastical approval
© 1987 Ignatius Press, San Francisco
Fourth printing 1989
All rights reserved
ISBN 0–89870–167–8
Library of Congress catalogue number 86–81472
Printed in the United States of America

"Thou shalt love the Lord thy God with thy whole heart, with thy whole soul and with thy whole mind" (Dt 6:5).

This is the commandment of our great God, and He cannot command the impossible. Love is a fruit in season at all times and within the reach of every hand. Anyone may gather it and no limit is set. Everyone can reach this love through meditation, spirit of prayer, and sacrifice, by an intense inner life.

—Mother Teresa of Calcutta

CONTENTS

LENT

EASTER

Contents

PENTECOST

INTRODUCTION

This is a book about love—God's love for us and our need to love one another. The words of the daily meditations are Mother Teresa's, but her inspiration comes from the One who is love.

Mother Teresa of Calcutta and the Order which she founded, the Missionaries of Charity, are living examples of God's love in action. In their work with the poor around the world, they show us the joy of loving, of seeing God in every person, of being one with God through prayer and sacrifice and service. Mother Teresa reminds us that we are all created in His image to love and to be loved.

When I first asked Mother Teresa in January 1986 for permission to compile this book of daily meditations, she sent a message to me through Sr. M. Frederick, M.C.: "Tell her to make it a prayer." I have tried to make this book a prayer. It is through prayer that we are brought closer to God, to His love for us and to His love within us. "Everyone can reach this love through meditation, spirit of prayer, and sacrifice, by an intense inner life", says Mother Teresa. It is my prayer that you who read her words in these daily meditations will be inspired to share the joy of loving with everyone you meet, first in your own home, then in your own neighborhood, school or work place each and every day of the year.

ACKNOWLEDGMENTS

The material for this book has come from many sources: books written about Mother Teresa, other books of her meditations and reflections, interviews, talks given by Mother Teresa and unpublished material supplied by the Missionaries of Charity and Co-Workers of Mother Teresa. I am thankful for the contributions so many have made in sharing Mother Teresa's words and works of love.

In addition, I would like especially to thank Sr. M. Sylvia, M.C., for her help in supplying material, encouragement and prayers; Fr. Steve Meyer, C.Ss.R., and Rev. James Gaderlund for their assistance in choosing themes consistent with the liturgical year; Frances M. Hunt, whose knowledge of Scripture was an invaluable aid; and Michael Collopy, Joan Daschbach and the Missionary of Charity Brothers for their contributions of photographs.

Finally, I wish to express my appreciation to my family for their constant love and support and to dedicate this book to them: to my husband, Jim, and to our two children, Julie and Daniel, whose love makes every season beautiful for me.

Dorothy S. Hunt

ADVENT

The people that walked in darkness have seen a great light. They that dwell in the land of the shadow of death, upon them hath the light shined. . . . For unto us a child is born, unto us a son is given (Is 9:2, 6).

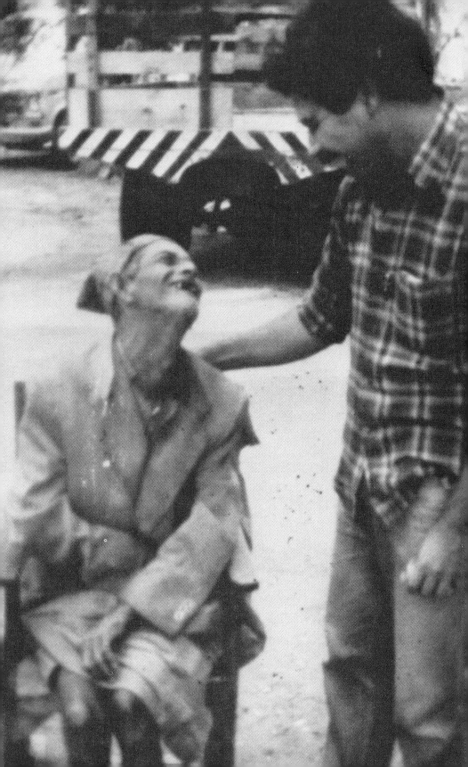

FAITH

"What matters is faith that makes its power felt through love" (Gal 5:6).

FIRST SUNDAY OF ADVENT

A gift of God

Faith is a gift of God. Without it there would be no life. And our work, to be fruitful, and to be all for God, and to be beautiful, has to be built on faith—faith in Christ, who has said, "I was hungry, I was naked, I was sick and I was homeless, and you ministered to Me." On these words of His all our work is based (GG, 15).

MONDAY

To see Christ in the poor

We need the eyes of deep faith to see Christ in the broken body and dirty clothes under which the most beautiful One among the sons of men hides. We shall need the hands of Christ to touch those bodies wounded by pain and suffering.

How pure our hands must be if we have to touch

Christ's Body as the priest touches Him in the appearance of bread at the altar. With what love and devotion and faith he lifts the sacred Host! These same feelings we too must have when we lift the body of the sick poor (LC, 109).

TUESDAY

Faith, a gospel of love

Our holy faith is nothing but a gospel of love, revealing to us God's love for men and claiming in return man's love for God (LC, 102).

WEDNESDAY

Become a child in God's hands

"Unless you become a little child . . . " I am sure you will understand beautifully everything if you would only "become" a little child in God's hands. Your longing for God is so deep, and yet He keeps Himself away from you. He must be forcing Himself to do so, because He loves you so much—as to give Jesus to die for you and for me. Christ is longing to be your Food. Surrounded with fullness of living Food, you allow yourself to starve. The personal love Christ has for you is infinite; the small difficulty you have regarding His Church is finite. Overcome the finite with the infinite. Christ has created you because He wanted you. I know what you feel—terrible longing with dark emptiness. And yet, He is the one in love with you (SB, 142).

THURSDAY

Why faith is lacking

Faith is lacking because there is so much selfishness and so much gain only for self. But faith, to be true, has to be a giving love. Love and faith go together. They complete each other (GG, 16).

People don't know they have lost their faith. If they were convinced that the person lying in the dirt is their brother or sister, I believe they would do something for that person. People don't know what compassion is. They don't know people. If they understood, they would immediately realize the greatness of the people lying in the street and would simply love them. And the love would surely lead them to place themselves at their service (AP, 109–110).

FRIDAY

Fruit of faith

Faith in action is love and love in action is service—therefore "the way of life" is but the fruit of faith—faith has to be put in action of love if it has to live—and love to be true and living—to be God's love in action—must be service . . . (ML, 160).

SATURDAY

Not called to be successful

We do nothing. He does everything. All glory must be returned to Him.

God has not called me to be successful. He called me to be faithful (MLP, 98).

HUMILITY

"Behold, I am the handmaid of the Lord; let it be to me according to your word" (Lk 1:38).

SECOND SUNDAY OF ADVENT

A Child in need of His mother

[Advent] is like springtime. He comes like a little child so much in need of His mother. Let us see and touch the greatness that fills the depth of their humility, Jesus' and Mary's. If we really want God to fill us we must empty ourselves through humility of all that is selfishness in us (LC, 85).

MONDAY

To be a handmaiden

May our Mother be a mother to each one of us and so the cause of our joy. And may each one of us be Jesus to her and so become the cause of her joy. No one learned the lesson of humility as well as Mary did. She was the handmaiden. To be a handmaiden is to be at someone's disposal—to be used according to someone's wish—with full trust and joy. Cheerfulness and joy were Our Lady's strength. Only joy could have given her the strength to go in haste over the hills of Judea to do the work of handmaiden to her cousin. So let us go in haste over the hills of difficulties (LC, 89).

TUESDAY

Learn from Our Lady

How much we can learn from Our Lady. She was so humble because she was all for God. She was full of grace and she made use of the almighty power that was in her—the grace of God.

The most beautiful part of Our Lady was that, when Jesus came into her life, immediately she went in haste to Elizabeth to give Jesus to her and her son. And we read in the Gospel that the child "leapt with joy" at this first contact with Christ. Our Lady was the most wonderful wire. She allowed God to fill her to the brim, so by her surrender, "be it unto me according to thy word", she became full of grace which she went to pass on to John. So let us ask God to use us now to go round the world, especially in our own communities, and continue connecting the wires of the hearts of men to the current, Jesus (LS, 22).

WEDNESDAY

Humility of Christ

It is beautiful to see the humility of Christ. This humility can be seen in the crib, in the exile in Egypt, in the hidden life, in the inability to make people understand Him, in the desertion of His apostles, in the hatred of the Jews and all the terrible sufferings and death of His Passion and now in His permanent state of humility in the Tabernacle, where He has reduced Himself to such a small particle of bread that the priest can hold Him with two fingers (LS, 48).

THURSDAY

God is truly humble

In God I find two things admirable: His goodness and His humility. His love and His humility are striking. God is truly humble; He comes down and uses instruments as weak and imperfect as we are. He deigns to work through us. Is that not marvelous? (MTC, 141).

If it was not for God's tender love, every moment of the day, we would be nothing. We are nothing from the point of view of the world. The humility of God is to use you and me for His great work—so that we will share in the great vocation of belonging to Jesus. Christ came to bring the Good News that the Father loves each one of us with a personal love (SV, 259).

FRIDAY

Do the humble work

We must not drift away from the humble works, because these are the works nobody will do. It is never too small. We are so small we look at things in a small way. But God, being Almighty, sees everything great. Therefore, even if you write a letter for a blind man or you just go and sit and listen, or you take the mail for him, or you visit somebody or bring a flower to somebody—small things—or wash clothes for somebody, or clean the house. Very humble work that is where you and I must be. For there are many people who can do big things. But there are very few people who will do the small things (LS, 49).

SATURDAY

Welcome Jesus at Christmas

Let us pray that we shall be able to welcome Jesus at Christmas not in the cold manger of our heart but in a heart full of love and humility, a heart warm with love for one another (LS, 74).

TRUST

" . . . Behold, an angel of the Lord appeared to him in a dream, saying, 'Joseph, son of David, do not fear to take Mary your wife, for that which is conceived in her is of the Holy Spirit.' . . . When Joseph woke from sleep, he did as the angel of the Lord commanded him; he took his wife, but he knew her not until she had borne a son; and he called His name Jesus" (Mt 1:20, 24–25).

THIRD SUNDAY OF ADVENT

Trust and believe

Trust God. Feel the security of divine providence. Trust Him. He knows. He will provide. Let Him test and trust our faith in Him. Wait on Him. Trust and believe (MLP, 103).

MONDAY

You will not let me down

My God, You, only You. I trust in Your call, Your inspiration. You will not let me down (MLP, 10).

TUESDAY

Allow God to make future plans

The future is not in our hands. We have no power over it. We can act only today. We have a sentence in our Constitutions that says: ". . . We will allow the good God to make plans for the future—for yesterday has gone, tomorrow has not yet come and we have only today to make Him known, loved and served" (No. 22). Our Lord told us not to fret about tomorrow, which is in God's hands. So we do not worry about it. Then Jesus is the same yesterday, today and tomorrow. Jesus is the same. He is the same today and tomorrow, and only He matters (MTC, 262–263).

WEDNESDAY

Jesus never deceives

We are able to go through the most terrible places fearlessly, because Jesus in us will never deceive us; Jesus in us is our love, our strength, our joy and our compassion (MTC, 160).

THURSDAY

God showed us what to do

In the choice of works, there was neither planning nor preconceived ideas. We started our work as the suffering of the people called us. God showed us what to do (SV, 44).

FRIDAY

Give Jesus your hands and your heart

Give Jesus not only your hands to serve, but your heart to love. Pray with absolute trust in God's loving care for you. Let Him use you without consulting you. Let Jesus fill you with joy that you may preach without preaching (Unpub.).

SATURDAY

One thing Jesus asks

One thing Jesus asks of me is that I lean upon Him; that in Him alone I put complete trust; that I surrender myself to Him unreservedly (LC, 103–104).

LOVE BEGINS AT HOME

"And she gave birth to her first-born Son and wrapped Him in swaddling cloths, and laid Him in a manger, because there was no place for them in the inn" (Lk 2:7).

FOURTH SUNDAY OF ADVENT

Christ comes like a little child

At Christmas Christ comes like a little child, so small, so helpless, so much in need of all that love can give. Are we ready to receive Him: If Mary and Joseph were looking for a place to make a home for Jesus, would they choose our house and all that it holds and is filled with? (LS, 71).

MONDAY

Where love begins

. . . Where does love begin? At home. . . .

Let us learn to love in our family. In our own family we may have very poor people and we do not notice them. We have no time to smile, no time to talk to each other. Let us bring that love, that tenderness into our own home and you will see the difference (IT, no. 4).

TUESDAY

Make your home another Nazareth

Make your house, your family, another Nazareth where love, peace, joy and unity reign, for love begins at home. You must start there and make your home the center of burning love. You must be the hope of eternal happiness to your wife, your husband, your child, to your grandfather, grandmother, to whoever is connected with you (LS, 71).

WEDNESDAY

Called to serve at home

. . . Love starts at home and lasts at home, and there is constantly scope for it there; the home is each one's first field of loving, devotion and service. Begin to speak to people who talk your own language and share your culture, but to whom you never addressed a word previously.

Indeed, we are not to be often traveling to Jericho. Our main job is in the holy city of our birth, our own Jerusalem, where the temple of the true God stands. There we are called to serve Him in our brethren, in our house and in the next-door neighbors. . . .

Do you know the members of your family, of your locality? Do you care for them, do you try to make them happy? First do that and then you may think of the poor of India and of other areas (MTC, 185).

THURSDAY

No time for family life

. . . Jesus became a child to teach us to love the child. In the eyes of the child, I see the spirit of life, of God.

We must make sacrifices to protect life. But family life is broken. There is hunger for more things. People need more cars, more machines. There is no time for family life. When Prime Minister Nehru came to open our Shishu Bhavan, our Children's Home in Delhi, he looked at the abandoned children we had taken in. He said, "Take care of these children. One of them may be a Prime Minister one day" (SV, 391).

FRIDAY

Will He find a warm heart?

At this Christmas when Christ comes, will He find a warm heart? Mark the season of Advent by loving and serving the others with God's own love and concern (Unpub.).

SATURDAY

Home to the homeless Christ

To offer a home to the homeless Christ start by making your own homes places where peace, happiness and love abound, through your love for each member of your family and for your neighbors (SMT, 61).

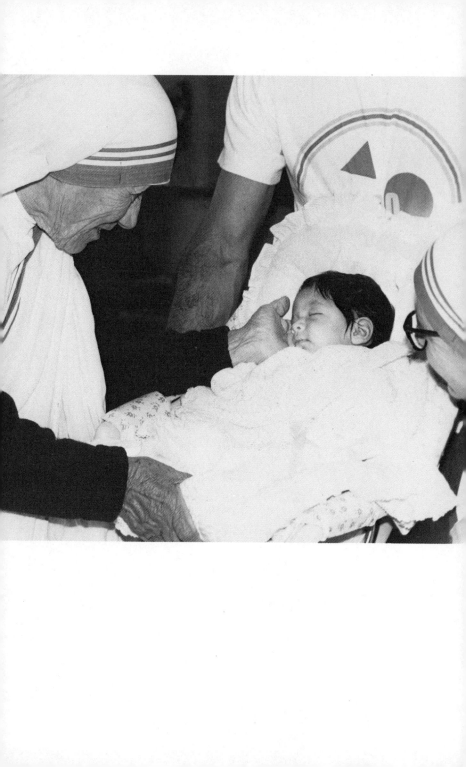

CHRISTMAS

(Christmas Day, December 25)

And the angel said to them, "Be not afraid; for behold, I bring you good news of a great joy which will come to all the people; for to you is born this day in the city of David a Savior, who is Christ the Lord. And this will be a sign for you: you will find a babe wrapped in swaddling cloths and lying in a manger." And suddenly there was with the angel a multitude of the heavenly host praising God and saying, "Glory to God in the highest, and on earth peace among men with whom He is pleased!" (Lk 2:10–14).

THE FAMILY

"The shepherds went in haste to Bethlehem and found Mary and Joseph, and the Baby lying in a manger" (Lk 2:16).

FIRST SUNDAY AFTER CHRISTMAS

No time to enjoy

I think the world today is upside down, and is suffering so much, because there is so very little love in the homes and in family life. We have no time for our children, we have no time for each other; there is no time to enjoy each other. If we could only bring back into our lives the life that Jesus, Mary and Joseph lived in Nazareth, if we could make our homes another Nazareth, I think that peace and joy would reign in the world (GG, 11).

MONDAY

Mothers, the heart of the home

Mothers are the heart of the home; they build family life by wanting, loving and taking care of their children. . . .

Recently, in L———, a young woman of twenty-one years, who had been scolded in the morning, attempted suicide later in the day by swallowing kerosene. Taken to the hospital, she said to the priest: "My mother chased me out of the house and I did not know where to go; so I thought the best thing would be to kill myself."

Much suffering of young people is attributable to the family and particularly to mothers. Mothers make the home a center of love. Their role is sometimes hard, but there is the example of the Blessed Virgin, who teaches us to be good with our children. We Missionaries of Charity also have to be mothers and make our communities happy homes (LC, 24).

TUESDAY

Home is where the mother is

The home is where the mother is. Once I picked up a child and took him to our Children's Home, gave him a bath, clean clothes, everything, but after a day the child ran away. He was found again by somebody else but again he ran away. Then I said to the Sisters: "Please follow that child. One of you stay with him and see where he goes when he runs away." And the child ran away the third time. There under a tree was the mother. She had put two stones under a small earthenware vessel and was cooking something that she had picked up from the dustbins. The Sister asked the child: "Why did you run away from the home?" And the child said: "But this is my home because this is where my mother is."

Mother was there. That was home. That the food was

taken from the dustbin was all right because mother had cooked it. It was mother that hugged the child, mother who wanted the child and the child had its mother. Between a wife and a husband it is the same (LS, 72–73).

WEDNESDAY

Understanding love

You and I, being women, we have this tremendous thing in us, understanding love. I see that so beautifully in our people, in our poor women, who day after day, and every day, meet suffering, accept suffering for the sake of their children. I have seen parents, mothers, going without so many things, so many things, even resorting to begging, so that the children may have what they need.

I have seen a mother holding to her handicapped child because that child is her child. She had an understanding love for the suffering of her child. I remember a woman who had twelve children, and the first of them was terribly disabled, terribly handicapped. I cannot describe to you what the child looked like, mentally, physically, and I offered her to take that child into our home where we have so many like that; and she started crying and she said to me, "Mother, don't say that, don't say that. She is the greatest gift of God to me and my family. All our love is centered on this child. Our life would be empty if you took her away from us. . . ."

Do we have that kind of understanding love today?

Do we recognize that in our homes, my child, my husband, my wife, my father, my mother, my sister, my brother, needs that understanding, that handshake? (MTC, 222–223).

THURSDAY

That little unborn child

And today, we look to the world and see that little one, that unborn child, has become the target of death, the target of destruction, of destroying, of killing. And to think that God says, even if a mother could forget—but it is impossible for a mother to forget. But even if a mother could forget, I will not forget you.

And yet today, the mother forgets her child. Not only forgets it, but destroys it. And for what? The mother is afraid of the child, of that little unborn child . . . the most beautiful creation of God's love . . . the gift of God.

And so today, let us thank God that our parents loved us. Thank God. Let us pray today that every mother will want her child. That no mother will use means to destroy it. That no mother will have that feeling of not wanting the unborn child. That no mother will be afraid to feed one more child, to educate one more child, to take care of one more child (RL, 3, 5).

FRIDAY

(or Solemnity of Mary, January 1)

Mary, the Mother of God

Mary is the Mother of God, Mother of Jesus and our Mother, Mother of the Church.

She is the Mother of the whole world because when the angel gave her the news, the Good News, that she would become the Mother of Christ, it was at that time, by accepting to become the handmaid of the Lord, that she accepted to be our Mother also, for the whole of mankind. Mother Mary is the hope of mankind.

She has given us Jesus . . . (GG, 47–48).

SATURDAY

Christ, the Head of the family

Christ is the Head of this family, the silent listener at every conversation, the unseen guest at every meal (Unpub.).

CHRIST COMES IN THE POOR

"He was in the world, and the world was made through Him, yet the world knew Him not. He came to His own home, and His own people received Him not" (Jn 1:10–11).

"I was hungry and you gave Me food, I was thirsty and you gave Me drink, I was a stranger and you welcomed Me, I was naked and you clothed Me, I was sick and you visited Me, I was in prison and you came to Me" (Mt 25:35–36).

SECOND SUNDAY AFTER CHRISTMAS

Do we pass Him by?

Today, once more, when Jesus comes amongst His own, His own don't know Him! He comes in the rotten bodies of our poor; He comes even in the rich choked by their own riches. He comes in the loneliness of their hearts, and when there is no one to love them. Jesus comes to you and me and often, very, very often, we pass Him by (LS, 10).

MONDAY

Suffering of Jesus

After working many years among the dying, the sick, the crippled, the handicapped and mentally deficient men, women and children, I have come to one conclusion only. As I have tried to feel with the people their suffering, I have come to the understanding of what Jesus felt when He came amongst His own and they didn't want Him.

Today Christ is in people who are unwanted, unemployed, uncared for, hungry, naked and homeless. They seem useless to the state or to society and nobody has time for them. It is you and I as Christians, worthy of the love of Christ if our love is true, who must find them and help them. They are there for the finding (LS, 10).

TUESDAY

Christ's hunger for love

When Christ said, "I was hungry and you fed Me", He didn't mean only the hunger for bread and for food; He also meant the hunger to be loved. Jesus Himself experienced this loneliness. He came amongst His own and His own received Him not, and it hurt Him then and it has kept on hurting Him. The same hunger, the same loneliness, the same having no one to be accepted by and to be loved and wanted by. Every human being in that case resembles Christ in His loneliness; and that is the hardest part, that's real hunger (GG, 30–31).

WEDNESDAY

"A Christian is giving"

Some time ago, a Hindu gentleman was asked: "What is a Christian?" And he gave a very simple and a very strange answer: "A Christian is giving." And right from the beginning we find that it is really just giving. God loved the world so much that He gave His Son—the first great giving. Being rich He became poor for you and me. He gave Himself totally. But that was not enough. He wanted to give something more—to give us the chance to give to Him. So He made Himself the hungry one, the naked one so that we could give to Him (LS, 53).

THURSDAY

Needs of the poor

Today, the poor are hungry for bread and rice—and for love and the living word of God.

The poor are thirsty—for water and peace, truth and justice.

The poor are homeless—for a shelter made of bricks, and for a joyful heart that understands, covers, loves.

The poor are naked—for clothes, for human dignity and compassion for the naked sinner.

They are sick—for medical care, and for that gentle touch and a warm smile (LS, 14).

FRIDAY

Jesus in everyone

Our work . . . calls for us to see Jesus in everyone. He has told us that He is the hungry one. He is the naked one. He is the thirsty one. He is the one without a home. He is the one who is suffering. These are our treasures. . . . They are Jesus. Each one is Jesus in His distressing disguise (SV, 50).

Hungry for love, He looks at you; thirsty for kindness, He begs from you; naked for loyalty, He hopes in you; sick and in prison for friendship, He wants from you; homeless for shelter in your heart, He asks of you. Will you be the one to Him? (Unpub.).

SATURDAY

Serving Christ in the poor

The "shut-in", the unwanted, the unloved, the alcoholics, the dying destitutes, the abandoned and the lonely, the outcasts and the untouchables, the leprosy sufferers—all those who are a burden to human society—who have lost all hope and faith in life—who have forgotten how to smile—who have lost the sensibility of the warm hand-touch of love and friendship—they look to us for comfort. If we turn our back on them, we turn it on Christ, and at the hour of our death we shall be judged if we have recognized Christ in them, and on what we have done for and to them. There will only be two ways, "come" and "go".

Therefore, I appeal to every one of you—poor and rich, young and old—to give your own hands to serve Christ in His poor and your hearts to love Him in them. They may be far or near, materially poor or spiritually poor, hungry for love and friendship, ignorant of the riches of the love of God for them, homeless for want of a home made of love in your heart; and since love begins at home maybe Christ is hungry, naked, sick or homeless in your own heart, in your family, in your neighbors, in the country you live in, in the world (LS, 14–15).

EPIPHANY

(January 6)

When they saw the star, they rejoiced exceedingly with great joy; and going into the house they saw the Child with Mary His Mother, and they fell down and worshiped Him. Then, opening their treasures, they offered Him gifts, gold and frankincense and myrrh. And being warned in a dream not to return to Herod, they departed to their own country by another way (Mt 2:10–12).

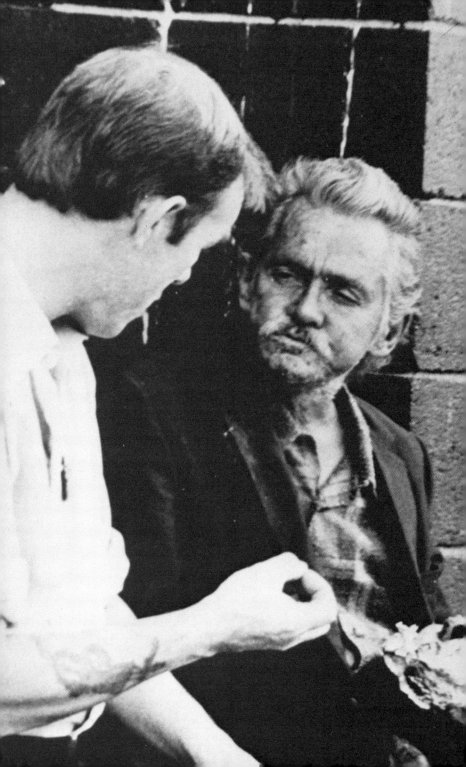

CONVERSION

"In those days Jesus came from Nazareth of Galilee and was baptized by John in the Jordan" (Mk 1:9).

FIRST SUNDAY AFTER EPIPHANY

To convert is to bring to Christ

To convert is to bring to God. To sanctify is to fill with God. To convert and sanctify is the work of God, but God has chosen in His great mercy the Missionaries of Charity to help Him in His own work. It is a special grace granted to the Missionaries of Charity with no merit on their part to carry the light of Christ into the dark holes and slums (LC, 99).

MONDAY

I hope to convert hearts

Oh, I hope I am converting. I don't mean what you think. I hope we are converting hearts. Not even Almighty God can convert a person unless that person wants it. What we are all trying to do by our work, by serving the people, is to come closer to God. If in coming face to face with God we accept Him in our lives, then we are converting. We become a better Hindu, a better Muslim, a better Catholic, a better whatever we are, and then by being better we come closer and closer to Him. If we accept Him fully in our lives, then that is conversion. What approach would I use? For me, naturally, it would be a Catholic one, for you it may be Hindu, for someone else, Buddhist, according to one's conscience. What God is in your mind you must accept. But I cannot prevent myself from trying to give you what I have (HP, 136).

TUESDAY

Conversion cannot be forced

I am not afraid to say I am in love with Jesus because He is everything to me. But you may have a different picture in your life. And this is the way that conversion has to be understood—people think that conversion is just changing overnight. It is not like that. Nobody, not even your father and mother, can make you do that. Not even Almighty God can force a person. Even Jesus, though He was God Himself, could not convert the hearts of the people unless they allowed Him to (HP, 136–137).

WEDNESDAY

Zeal for souls

Zeal for souls is the effect and the proof of true love of God. We cannot but be consumed with the desire for saving souls. Zeal is the test of love and the test of zeal is devotedness to His cause, spending life and energy in the work of souls . . . (LC, 99).

THURSDAY

Growing in Love

Our purpose is to take God and His love to the poorest of the poor, irrespective of their ethnic origin or the faith that they profess. Our discernment of aid is not the belief but the necessity. We never try to convert those who receive to Christianity but in our work we bear witness to the love of God's presence and if Catholics, Protestants, Buddhists or agnostics become for this reason better men—simply better—we will be satisfied. Growing up in love they will be nearer to God and will find Him in His goodness (LS, 81).

FRIDAY

"The treasure I have . . ."

. . . The treasure I have, I want to give to you, but I cannot. I can pray for you that you may have the courage to receive it, because faith is a gift of God, that great gift of God that He has given to us in Holy Communion, to satisfy our hunger, because we have been created in the image of God (MLP, 99).

SATURDAY

"Face to face"

It matters to the individual what Church he belongs to. If that individual thinks and believes that this is the only way to God for him, this is the way God comes into his life. If he does not know any other way and if he has no doubt so that he does not need to search then this is his way to salvation. This is the way God comes into his life. But the moment a soul has the grace to know and to want to know more about God, more about faith, more about religion, then he has to search and if he does not search then he goes astray. God gives to every soul that He has created a chance to come face to face with Him, to accept or reject Him (LS, 82).

THOUGHTFULNESS
KINDNESS

"They have no wine" (Jn 2:3).

SECOND SUNDAY AFTER EPIPHANY

Thoughtfulness, the beginning of holiness

Thoughtfulness, the kindly regard for others, is the beginning of holiness. If you learn the art of being thoughtful, you will be more and more like Christ; His heart was kind and gentle, and He always thought of others. Our vocation, to be beautiful, must be full of regard for others. Jesus did good wherever He went. Our Lady at Cana thought only of the needs of others and told Jesus about them (LC, 34–35).

MONDAY

The abode of God Most High

The thoughtfulness of Jesus and Mary and Joseph was so great that it made Nazareth the abode of God Most

High. If we also have that kind of thoughtfulness for each other, our homes would really become the abode of God Most High (LS, 33).

TUESDAY

Love or violence from the tongue

The quickest and the surest way [toward thoughtfulness] is the "tongue"—use it for the good of others. If you think well of others, you will also speak well of others and to others. From the abundance of the heart the mouth speaketh. If your heart is full of love, you will speak of love.

Violence of the tongue is very real—sharper than any knife, wounding and creating bitterness that only the grace of God can heal (LS, 33).

WEDNESDAY

Kindness of Mary

Mary can teach us kindness—she went in haste to serve Elizabeth. "They have no wine", she told Jesus at Cana. Let us, like her, be aware of the needs of the poor, be they spiritual or material, and let us, like her, give generously of the love and grace we are granted (LS, 22).

Be kind and merciful. Let no one ever come to you without leaving better and happier. Be the living expression of God's kindness—kindness in your face, kindness in your eyes, kindness in your smile, kindness in your warm greeting (LS, 42).

THURSDAY

*Mistakes done out of kindness preferred to
miracles performed with unkindness*

Be true Co-Workers of Christ. Radiate and live His life. Be an angel of comfort to the sick, a friend to the little ones, and love each other as God loves each one of you with a special, most intense love. Be kind to each other in your homes. Be kind to those who surround you. I prefer that you make mistakes in kindness rather than that you work miracles in unkindness. Often just one word, one look, one quick action, and darkness fills the heart of the one we love (SV, 324).

FRIDAY

Hindu family sharing

I'll never forget one night a man came to our place and said, "There's a family, for a long time—with eight children—with nothing to eat. Do something." And so

I brought some rice for the family, and I could see the terrible hunger on the children's faces. And the mother divided the rice and she went out.

When she came back, I said, "Where did you go? What did you do?" And she said very beautifully, "They are hungry also." I was not surprised that she gave, but I was very surprised that she *knew,* that she knew about this family. They were a Hindu family and their neighbor was a Muslim family. And yet she knew that they were suffering, that they were also hungry. In her suffering, a terrible suffering—seeing her children really dying of hunger—still, she had the joy and the love and the courage to share before she gave to her own children.

This is something that we have to more and more and more have—that concern—concern first in our families—our husband, our wife, our children (Talk 3).

SATURDAY

Thoughtfulness and kindness of God

God is taking care of His poor people through us. He has shown such thoughtfulness and kindness to our people in so many small details! . . . If I wrote or spoke for hours and hours, I would be able to give thousands of proofs of the delicate kindness and thoughtfulness of God (MLP, 53).

BELONGING TO JESUS

"And He said to them, 'Follow Me, and I will make you fishers of men.' Immediately they left their nets and followed Him" (Mt 4:19–20).

THIRD SUNDAY AFTER EPIPHANY

Our vocation to belong to Jesus

. . . It is not our vocation to serve the poorest of the poor; our vocation is to belong to Jesus with the conviction that nothing and nobody can separate us from the love of Christ (CW, no. 26).

Christ chooses us

"You have not chosen Me; I have chosen you" (Jn 15:16). It is Christ's choice for us that makes us what we are. . . . He will work out His plan in us and through us in spite of any failure we may meet . . . (Unpub.).

MONDAY

Radiate the joy of belonging to God

Make every effort to walk in the presence of God, to see God in everyone you meet and to live your morning meditation throughout the day. In the streets in particular, radiate the joy of belonging to God, of living with Him and being His. For this reason, in the streets, in the shelters, in your work, you should always be praying with all your heart and soul (LC, 9–10).

All of us have been called. . . . The fact that you have been given a gift may constitute a call (SV, 409).

TUESDAY

"Wherever God has put you, that is your vocation"

So for all of us, it doesn't matter what we do or where we are as long as we remember that we belong to Him, that we are His, that we are in love with Him. The means He gives us, whether we are working for the rich or we are working for the poor, whether we are working with high-class people or low-class people, it makes no difference; but how much love we are putting into the work we do is what matters (MLP, 87).

WEDNESDAY

Vocation to work for lepers?

A few weeks back, one of our Brothers came to me in distress and said, "My vocation is to work for the lepers. [He loves the lepers.] I want to spend all my life, my everything in this vocation."

I said to him, "You are making a mistake, Brother. Your vocation is to belong to Jesus. He has chosen you for Himself and the work is only a means of your love for Him in action. Therefore it does not matter what work you are doing, but the main thing is that you belong to Him, that you are His and that He gives you the means to do this for Him" (MLP, 87).

THURSDAY

All we do is for Jesus

All we do—our prayer, our work, our suffering—is for Jesus. Our life has no other reason or motivation.

This is a point many people do not understand.

I serve Jesus twenty-four hours a day. Whatever I do is for Him. And He gives me strength.

I love Him in the poor and the poor in Him. But always the Lord comes first.

Whenever a visitor comes to our house, I take him to the chapel to pray awhile. I tell him, "Let us first greet the Master of the house. Jesus is here."

It is for Him we work, to Him we devote ourselves. He gives us the strength to carry on this life and to do so with happiness.

Without Him we could not do what we do. We certainly could not continue doing it for a whole lifetime. One year, two years, perhaps; but not during a whole life, without thought of reward, without expectation of anything good except to suffer with Him who loved us so much that He gave His life for us.

Without Jesus our life would be meaningless, incomprehensible.

Jesus explains our life (MLP, 25–26).

FRIDAY

I belong to Christ

I am Albanian by birth. Now I am a citizen of India. I am also a Catholic nun. In my work, I belong to the whole world. But in my heart, I belong to Christ (MLP, 1).

SATURDAY

Accept whatever He gives; give whatever He takes

Keep giving Jesus to your people, not by words, but by your example, by your being in love with Jesus, by radiating His holiness and spreading His fragrance of love everywhere you go. Just keep the joy of Jesus as your strength. Be happy and at peace. Accept whatever He gives—and give whatever He takes with a big smile. You belong to Him. Tell Him, "I am Yours, and if You cut me to pieces, every single piece will be only all Yours." Let Jesus be the victim and the priest in you (GG, 38–39).

WHO ARE THE POOR

"Blessed are you poor, for yours is the kingdom of God" (Lk 6:20).

FOURTH SUNDAY AFTER EPIPHANY

The poor are great people!

The poor are great people!

We must love them, not by feeling pity for them. We must love them because it is Jesus in the distressing disguise of the poor. They are our brothers and sisters. They are our people. Those lepers, those dying, those hungry, those naked: they are Jesus! (MLP, 92).

MONDAY

Those whom society rejects

The poor people whom we gather each day are those whom society rejects and abandons. We try to give human dignity back to these people. As children of God they have a right to it (MTC, 221).

TUESDAY

How much we owe the poor!

We must acknowledge the dignity of the poor, respect them, esteem them, love them, serve them. . . . We owe a debt of gratitude to the poor. The poor people are great people, most lovable people. Often I think they are the ones to whom we owe our greatest gratitude. They teach us by their faith, their resignation, their patience in suffering. They allow us to help them. And doing so, we are serving Jesus (MTC, 220).

Only in heaven will we see how much we owe to the poor for helping us to love God better because of them (MLP, 97).

WEDNESDAY

Do we know the poor?

We come across people who are only known by their address number. Do we really realize that such people exist? Perhaps across the street. It might be a blind person who would be happy if we volunteered to read the newspaper. It might even be someone rich who has no one to visit. The rich person has a lot of things, but he is smothered by them. He lacks human contact and that is what that person needs (AP, 108).

THURSDAY

Extraordinary personalities of the poor

The poor, the lepers, the dispossessed, the neglected and even the alcoholics we serve are all great people. Many of them have extraordinary personalities. We should communicate this experience, which comes from serving them, to those who do not have or have never had such a beautiful possibility. It is one of the greatest comforts in our work (AP, 106).

FRIDAY

Looking toward the door

Where are the old people today? They are put in institutions. Why? Because they are unwanted, they are a burden. I remember some time ago I visited a very wonderful home for old people. There were about forty there and they had everything, but they were all looking towards the door. There was not a smile on their faces, and I asked the Sister in charge of them: "Sister, why are these people not smiling? Why are they looking towards the door?" And she, very beautifully, had to answer and give the truth: "It's the same every day. They are longing for someone to come and visit them." This is great poverty (LS, 72).

It isn't necessary to go out to the slums to find a lack of love and poverty. There is someone who suffers in every family and in every neighborhood (SMT, 53).

SATURDAY

The poor are the hope of the world

The poor are God's gift; they are our love. Christ will not ask how much we did but how much love we put into what we did. There are many people who are spiritually poor. The spiritual poverty found in Europe, in America, is a heavy burden to bear. In these countries it is very difficult to convey a sense of God's love. . . .

The poor are "hope". By their courage they truly represent the hope of the world. They have taught us a different way of loving God by making us do our utmost to help them (LC, 23).

LIGHT OF THE WORLD

"You are the light of the world" (Mt 5:14).

FIFTH SUNDAY AFTER EPIPHANY

If Christians truly lived their faith

Christians are light for each other and for the rest of the world. If we are Christians we have to reveal Christ. Gandhi once said that if Christians truly lived their Christianity, there would be no Hindus in India. This, therefore, is what everyone expects from us: that our Christianity be real (SMT, 70).

MONDAY

The current is God

Often you see small and big wires, new and old, cheap and expensive electric cables up—they alone are useless and until the current passes through them there will be no light. The wire is you and me. The current is God. We have the power to let the current pass through us and use us to produce the light of the world or we can refuse to be used and allow the darkness to spread. My prayer is with each of you and I pray that each one of you will be holy, and so spread God's love, everywhere you go. Let His light of truth be in every person's life so that God can continue loving the world through you and me. Put your heart into being a bright light (LS, 7).

TUESDAY

Drops of oil in the lamp

Do not imagine that love to be true must be extraordinary. No, what we need in our love is the continuity to love the One we love. See how a lamp burns, by the continual consumption of the little drops of oil. If there are no more of these drops in the lamp, there will be no light, and the Bridegroom has a right to say: "I do not know you."

My children, what are these drops of oil in our lamps? They are the little things of everyday life: fidelity, punctuality, little words of kindness, just a little thought for others, those little acts of silence, of look and thought, of word and deed. These are the very drops of love that make our religious life burn with so much light.

Do not search for Jesus in far off lands; He is not there. He is in you. Just keep the lamp burning and you will always see Him (LC, 73–74).

WEDNESDAY

The lamp still burns

In Melbourne I paid a visit to an old man no one knew existed. I saw that his room was in horrible condition and I wanted to clean it up, but he stopped me: "I'm all right." I kept quiet, and finally he let me go ahead. In his room was a beautiful lamp, covered with dust. I asked: "Why don't you light the lamp?" He replied: "What for? Nobody comes to see me, and I don't need a lamp." Then I said to him: "Will you light the lamp if the Sisters come to see you?" "Yes," he said, "if I hear a human voice, I will light it." The other day he sent me word: "Tell my friend that the lamp she lit in my life burns constantly" (LC, 31–32).

THURSDAY

Only the means can be given

I want very much people to come to know God, to love Him, to serve Him, for that is true happiness. And what I have I want everyone in the world to have. But it is their choice. If they have seen the light they can follow it. I cannot give them the light: I can only give the means (HP, 137).

FRIDAY

Keep light of Christ burning

Keep the light of Christ always burning in your heart,
for He alone is the Way to walk. He is the Life to live.
He is the Love to love (GG, 41).

SATURDAY

Be a bright light

Am I a dark light? A false light? A bulb without the
connection, having no current, therefore shedding no
radiance? Put your heart into being a bright light
(LC, 112).

FORGIVENESS

"So if you are offering your gift at the altar, and there remember that your brother has something against you, leave your gift there before the altar and go; first be reconciled to your brother and then come and offer your gift" (Mt 5:23–24).

SIXTH SUNDAY AFTER EPIPHANY

To love we must forgive

We know that if we really want to love we must learn to forgive (GG, 34).

MONDAY

Reconciliation begins with ourselves

. . . Reconciliation begins not first with others but with ourselves. It starts by having a clean heart within. A clean heart is able to see God in others. The tongue, the part of our body that comes in such close contact with the Body of Christ, can become an instrument of peace and joy or of sorrow and pain. . . . Forgive and ask to be forgiven; excuse rather than accuse . . . (LC, 95).

TUESDAY

"*My son did this to me*"

I remember also, once I picked up a woman from a dustbin and I knew she was dying. I took her out and took her to the convent. She kept on repeating the same words: "My son did this to me." Not once did she utter the words: "I'm hungry", "I'm dying", "I'm suffering". She just kept on repeating: "My son did this to me." It took me a long time to help her to say: "I forgive my son", before she died (LS, 72).

LENT

Beware of practicing your piety before men in order to be seen by them; for then you will have no reward from your Father who is in heaven.

Thus, when you give alms, sound no trumpet before you, as the hypocrites do in the synagogues and in the streets, that they may be praised by men. Truly, I say to you, they have their reward. But when you give alms, do not let your left hand know what your right hand is doing, so that your alms may be in secret; and your Father who sees in secret will reward you.

And when you pray, you must not be like the hypocrites; for they love to stand and pray in the synagogues and at the street corners, that they may be seen by men. Truly, I say to you, they have their reward. But when you pray, go into your room and shut the door and pray to your Father who is in secret; and your Father who sees in secret will reward you. . . .

And when you fast, do not look dismal, like the hypocrites, for they disfigure their faces that their fasting may be seen by men. Truly, I say to you, they have their reward. But when you fast, anoint your head and wash your face, that your fasting may not be seen by men but by your Father who is in secret; and your Father who sees in secret will reward you (Mt 6:1–6; 16–18).

SIN
FORGIVENESS

"Yet even now," says the Lord,
   "return to me with all your heart,
with fasting, with weeping, and with mourning;
   and rend your hearts and not your garments."
Return to the Lord, your God,
   for He is gracious and merciful,
slow to anger, and abounding in steadfast love,
   and repents of evil (Joel 2:12–13).

ASH WEDNESDAY

God cannot hate

God is purity Himself; nothing impure can come before Him, but I don't think God can hate, because God is love and God loves us in spite of our misery and sinfulness. He is our loving Father and so we have only to turn to Him. God cannot hate; God loves because He is love, but impurity is an obstacle to seeing God. This doesn't mean only the sin of impurity; but any attachment, anything that takes us away from God, anything that makes us less Christlike, any hatred, any uncharitableness is also impurity. If we are full of sin, God cannot fill us, because even God Himself cannot fill what is full. That's why we need forgiveness to become empty, and then God fills us with Himself (GG, 37–38).

THURSDAY

Look at the cross

Do I really know sin and look at the crucifix properly?
Looking at the cross we know how deep our sins are.
Take the cross in your hands and meditate. Jesus had
compassion on the sinners. Jesus did not condemn the
sinful woman. I, too, need to be forgiven (Unpub.).

FRIDAY

Bitterness to Jesus

When we give bitterness to one another, we give it to
Jesus. Let us examine ourselves and see when and how
bitterness entered our hearts. By whom was I made
bitter? Whose lives did I make bitter by my lack of love
and unkindness? Empty your heart of it all by a good,
sincere confession. Confession is nothing but standing
before Jesus like that sinful woman because I have caught
myself in sin. . . . I come to the confessional a sinner
with sin, but I leave a sinner without sin (Unpub.).

SATURDAY

Be sinless out of love not fear

I do not want that you do not sin because you fear hell
or Purgatory, but because you love Jesus (Unpub.).

PRAYER

Our Father who art in heaven
Hallowed be Thy name.
Thy kingdom come.
Thy will be done.
*   On earth as it is in heaven.*
Give us this day our daily bread;
And forgive us our debts,
*   As we also have forgiven our debtors;*
And lead us not into temptation,
*   But deliver us from evil (Mt 6:9–13).*

FIRST SUNDAY OF LENT

"Jesus, pray with me, pray in me"

During this Lent, let us improve our spirit of prayer and recollection. Let us free our minds from all that is not Jesus. If you find it difficult to pray, ask Him again and again, "Jesus, come into my heart, pray with me, pray in me—that I may learn from Thee how to pray" (SV, 377).

When the time comes and we cannot pray, it is very simple—let Jesus pray in us to the Father in the silence of our hearts. If we cannot speak, He will speak. If we cannot pray, He will pray. So let us give Him our inability and our nothingness (IN, 33).

MONDAY

Love to pray

Love to pray—feel the need to pray often during the day and take the trouble to pray. If you want to pray better, you must pray more. Prayer enlarges the heart until it is capable of containing God's gift of Himself. Ask and seek and your heart will grow big enough to receive Him and keep Him as your own (LS, 17).

TUESDAY

Prayer must come from the heart

Prayer to be fruitful must come from the heart and must be able to touch the heart of God. See how Jesus taught His disciples to pray. Call God your Father, praise and glorify His name. Do His will, ask for daily bread, spiritual and temporal, ask for forgiveness of your own sins and that we may forgive others—and also for the grace to be delivered from evil which is in us and around us (LS, 17–18).

WEDNESDAY

My secret is quite simple

My secret is quite simple. I pray and through my prayer I become one in love with Christ, and see that praying to Him is to love Him, and that means to fulfill His words. Remember the words of Saint Matthew's Gospel:

I was hungry and you gave Me no food,
I was thirsty and you gave Me no drink,
I was a stranger and you did not welcome Me,
naked and you did not clothe Me,
sick and in prison and you did not visit Me.

My poor ones in the world's slums are like the suffering Christ. In them God's Son lives and dies, and through them God shows me His true face. Prayer for me means becoming twenty-four hours a day at one with the will of Jesus to live for Him, through Him and with Him (LS, 1).

THURSDAY

Pray while you work

You should spend at least half an hour in the morning and an hour at night in prayer. You can pray while you work. Work doesn't stop prayer, and prayer doesn't stop work. It requires only that small raising of mind to Him. "I love You, God, I trust You, I believe in You, I need You now." Small things like that. They are wonderful prayers (HP, 146).

FRIDAY

Simply talking to God

Prayer is simply talking to God. He speaks to us; we listen. We speak to Him; He listens. A two-way process: speaking and listening. Say this prayer often: "Jesus, in my heart, I believe in Your tender love for me. I love You."

The more you pray, the easier it becomes. The easier it becomes, the more you'll pray (MLP, 104).

SATURDAY

Jesus is the prayer

In reality there is but one prayer, only one substantial prayer. Jesus Himself.

In your life Jesus comes as the Bread of Life to be eaten, to be consumed by you. This is how He loves you. Then He comes as the hungry one, the Other, hoping to be fed with the bread of your life, with your heart by loving, your hands by serving.

Jesus has drawn us to be souls of prayer.

Jesus is our prayer, and He is also the answer to our prayer. He has chosen to be Himself in us the living song of love, praise, adoration, thanksgiving, intercession and reparation to the Father in the name of the whole creation (Unpub.).

SILENCE

"Be still and know that I am God" (Ps 46:10).

SECOND SUNDAY OF LENT

Souls of prayer are souls of silence

It is very hard to pray if one does not know how. We must help ourselves to learn.

The most important thing is silence. Souls of prayer are souls of deep silence. We cannot place ourselves directly in God's presence without imposing upon ourselves interior and exterior silence. That is why we must accustom ourselves to stillness of the soul, of the eyes, of the tongue (LC, 8).

MONDAY

Jesus waits in silence

Silence gives us a new outlook on everything. We need silence to be able to touch souls. . . . Jesus is always waiting for us in silence. In that silence He will listen to us, there He will speak to our soul, and there we will hear His voice. Interior silence is very difficult but we must make the effort. In silence we will find new energy and true unity (LS, 19–20).

TUESDAY

Not what we say but what God says

God is the friend of silence. We need to find God, but we cannot find Him in noise, in excitement. See how nature, the trees, the flowers, the grass grow in deep silence. See how the stars, the moon and the sun move in silence.

The more we receive in our silent prayer, the more we can give in our active life. Silence gives us a new way of looking at everything. We need this silence in order to touch souls. The essential thing is not what we say but what God says to us and what He says through us (LC, 8–9).

WEDNESDAY

Silence most important in training of Sisters

Once I was asked by someone what I consider most important in the training of the Sisters. I answered:

Silence. Interior and exterior silence. Silence is essential in a religious house. The silence of humility, of charity, the silence of the eyes, of the ears, of the tongue. There is no life of prayer without silence.

Silence, and then kindness, charity; silence leads to charity, charity to humility. Charity among themselves, accepting one another when they are different; charity for union in a community. Charity leads to humility. We must be humble. It strikes me how God is humble. He humbled Himself. He who possessed the fullness of the Godhead took the form of a servant. Even today God shows His humility by making use of instruments as deficient as we are, weak, imperfect, inadequate instruments (MLP, 101–102).

THURSDAY

The fruit of silence

The fruit of silence is prayer. The fruit of prayer is faith. The fruit of faith is love. The fruit of love is service (Unpub.).

FRIDAY

Man needs silence

Man needs silence.

To be alone or together looking for God in silence. There it is that we accumulate the inward power which we distribute in action, put in the smallest duty and spend in the severest hardships that befall on us.

Silence came before creation, and the heavens were spread without a word.

Christ was born in the dead of night; and though there has been no power like His, "He did not strive nor cry, neither was His voice heard in the streets" (MLP, 101).

SATURDAY

True inner life

The true inner life makes the active life burn forth and consume everything. It makes us find Jesus in the dark holes of the slums, in the most pitiful miseries of the poor, in the God-Man naked on the Cross, mournful, despised by all, the man of suffering, crushed like a worm by the scourging and the crucifixion (LC, 110).

SURRENDER

"Take your son, your only son Isaac . . ." (Gen 22:2).

THIRD SUNDAY OF LENT

Jesus asks for surrender

One thing Jesus asks of me is that I lean upon Him; that in Him alone I put complete trust; that I surrender myself to Him unreservedly. I need to give up my own desires in the work of my perfection. Even when I feel as if I were a ship without a compass, I must give myself completely to Him. I must not attempt to control God's actions. I must not desire a clear perception of my advance along the road, nor know precisely where I am on the way of holiness. I ask Him to make a saint of me, yet I must leave to Him the choice of that saintliness itself and still more the choice of the means that lead to it (LC, 103–104).

MONDAY

If God owes nothing . . .

Total surrender consists in giving ourselves completely to God, because God has given Himself to us. If God owes nothing to us and is ready to impart to us no less than Himself, shall we answer with just a fraction of ourselves? I give up my own self and in this way induce God to live for me. Therefore to possess God we must allow Him to possess our souls (LC, 102).

TUESDAY

Submission as blessedness

In you today, Jesus wants to relive His complete submission to His Father. Allow Him to do so. It does not matter how you feel as long as He feels all right in you. . . . Submission for someone who is in love is more than a duty—it is a blessedness (Unpub.).

WEDNESDAY

My will power is my own

God has created all things. All the butterflies, the animals—the whole of nature He has created for us. To them He has not given the will power to choose. They have only an instinct. Animals can be very lovable and love very beautifully, but that is out of instinct. But the human being can choose. That is the one thing that God does not take from us. The will power, the power to will. I want to go to heaven and I will, with the grace of God. If I choose to commit sin and go to hell, that is my choice. God cannot force me otherwise. That's why when we become religious we give up that will power. That is why the sacrifice is so great: the vow of obedience is very difficult. Because in making that vow you surrender the only thing that is your own—your will power. Otherwise my health, my body, my eyes, my everything are all His and He can take them. I can fall, I can break, but my will power doesn't go like this. I must choose to give it and that is beautiful (HP, 143).

THURSDAY

Spirit of Missionaries of Charity

Let our lives give expression to the spirit of the Missionaries of Charity: total surrender to God with mutual trust and love for all. If we really receive this spirit, we will truly become Christ's Co-Workers—messengers of His love. This spirit should spring from your hearts and go out to your own families, neighborhoods, cities, countries and to the whole world (SMT, 19).

FRIDAY

Infallible when you obey

. . . The good God has given you His work. He wants you to do His work in His way. Failure or success mean nothing to Him, as long as you do His work according to His plan and His will. You are infallible when you obey. The devil tries his best to spoil the work of God and as he cannot do it directly to Him, he makes us do God's work in our way and this is where the devil gains and we lose (LC, 68).

SATURDAY

Let God use you without consulting you. . . .

Let God use you without consulting you.
Let the Lord catch you. . . . Let yourself be caught by Him and then let Him dispose of you utterly (SV, 328).

We are neither big nor small but what we are in the eyes of God, and as long as we surrender ourselves totally, then God can use us without consulting us. We like to be consulted, but letting Him use us without consultation is very good for us. We must accept emptiness, accept being broken to pieces, accept success or failure (IN, 86).

SUFFERING

" 'Rabbi, who sinned, this man or his parents, that he was born blind?' Jesus answered, 'It was not that this man sinned, or his parents, but that the works of God might be made manifest in him' " (Jn 9:2–3).

FOURTH SUNDAY OF LENT

Accepting the "gift" of suffering

Today the world is an "open Calvary". Mental and physical suffering is everywhere. Pain and suffering have to come into your life but remember pain, sorrow, suffering are but the kiss of Jesus—signs that you have come so close to Him that He can kiss you. Accept them as a gift—all for Jesus. You are really reliving the Passion of Christ so accept Jesus as He comes into your life—bruised, divided, full of pains and wounds (LS, 62).

MONDAY

Suffering is the kiss of Jesus

When I see people suffer, I feel so helpless! It's difficult, but the only way I find is to say, "God loves you."

I always connect this by saying to them, "It's a sign

that you have come so close to Jesus on the Cross that He can kiss you."

I remember I told this to a woman who was dying of cancer with her small children surrounding her. I didn't know which was the greater agony: the agony of leaving the children, or the agony of her body.

I told her, "This is a sign that you have got so close to Jesus on the Cross that He can share His Passion with you, He can kiss you."

She joined her hands and said, "Mother, please tell Jesus to stop kissing me." She understood so beautifully! (MLP, 77).

TUESDAY

Suffering from lack of peace in family

Today there is so much trouble in the world and I think that much of it begins at home. The world is suffering so much because there is no peace. There is no peace because there is no peace in the family and we have so many thousands and thousands of broken homes. We must make our homes centers of compassion and forgive endlessly and so bring peace (LS, 71).

WEDNESDAY

Why people have had to die of starvation

If sometimes our poor people have had to die of starvation, it is not because God didn't care for them, but because you and I didn't give, were not instruments of love in the hands of God, to give them that bread, to give them that clothing; because we did not recognize Him, when once more Christ came in distressing disguise—in the hungry man, in the lonely man, in the homeless child, and seeking for shelter (GG, 24).

. . . The suffering of some can be blamed on the greed of others (MTC, 273).

THURSDAY

The greatest suffering

There is much suffering in the world—very much. And the material suffering is suffering from hunger, suffering from homelessness, from all kinds of diseases, but I still think the greatest suffering is being lonely, feeling unloved, just having no one. I have come more and more to realize that it is being unwanted that is the worst disease that any human being can ever experience (CW, no. 27).

When all recognize that our suffering neighbor is God Himself, and when you draw the consequences from that fact—on that day, there will be no more poverty, and we—the Missionaries of Charity—will have no work to do (SV, 409).

FRIDAY

The streets of Calcutta lead to every man's door

The streets of Calcutta lead to every man's door, and the very pain, the very ruin of our Calcutta of the heart witness to the glory that once was and ought to be (Unpub.).

SATURDAY

Remember the Resurrection has to come

Suffering, if it is accepted together, borne together, is joy. Remember that the Passion of Christ ends always in the joy of the Resurrection of Christ, so when you feel in your own heart the suffering of Christ, remember the Resurrection has to come—the joy of Easter has to dawn. Never let anything so fill you with sorrow as to make you forget the joy of the Risen Christ (LS, 63).

Suffering in itself does not bring joy, but Christ as seen in suffering does . . . (IN).

SUFFERING AND REDEMPTION

"Behold the Lamb of God, who takes away the sin of the world!"
(Jn 1:29).

". . . For Thou wast slain and by Thy blood didst purchase for God men of every tribe and language, people and nation" (Rev 5:9).

FIFTH SUNDAY OF LENT

Suffering shared with Christ's passion

Suffering is increasing in the world today. People are hungry for something more beautiful, for something greater than people round about can give. There is a great hunger for God in the world today. Everywhere there is much suffering, but there is also great hunger for God and love for each other.

Suffering in itself is nothing; but suffering shared with Christ's Passion is a wonderful gift. Man's most beautiful gift is that he can share in the Passion of Christ. Yes, a gift and a sign of His love; because this is how His Father proved that He loved the world—by giving His Son to die for us (CW, no. 27).

MONDAY

Our second selves

Amongst our Co-Workers we have got sick and crippled people who very often cannot do anything to share in the work. So they adopt a Sister or a Brother, offering all their sufferings and all their prayers for that Brother or that Sister, who then involve the sick Co-Worker fully in whatever he or she does. The two become like one person, and they call each other their second self. I have a second self like this in Belgium, Jacqueline de Decker.

My very dear suffering sisters and brothers, be assured that every one of us claims your love before the throne of God, and there every day we offer you, or rather offer each other to Christ for souls. We, the Missionaries of Charity, how grateful we must be—you to suffer and we to work. We complete in each other what is lacking in our relationship with Christ. Your life of sacrifice is the chalice, or rather our vows are the chalice, and your suffering and work are the wine—the spotless heart. We stand together holding the same chalice, and so are able to satiate His burning thirst for souls (CW, no. 27).

TUESDAY

"How can a merciful God allow such suffering?"

("How can a merciful God", asked a newspaperman, "allow such suffering, children dying of hunger, people killed in earthquakes . . . What can you say to that?")

. . . All that suffering—where would the world be without it? It is innocent suffering, and that is the same as the suffering of Jesus. He suffered for us and all the innocent suffering is joined to His in the Redemption. It is co-redemption. That is helping to save the world from worse things (SV, 267).

WEDNESDAY

Intercession and innocent suffering

I often wonder that if innocent people did not suffer so much what would happen to the world? They are the ones who are interceding the whole time. Their innocence is so pleasing to God. By accepting suffering, they intercede for us (HP, 142).

THURSDAY

Suffering as part of Redemption

Without our suffering our work would just be social work, very good and helpful, but it would not be the work of Jesus Christ, not part of the Redemption. Jesus wanted to help us by sharing our life, our loneliness, our agony and death. All that He has taken upon Himself and has carried it into the darkest night. Only by being one with us has He redeemed us. We are allowed to do the same; all the desolation of the poor people, not only their material poverty, but their spiritual destitution must be redeemed, and we must share it, for only by being with them can we redeem them, that is by bringing God into their lives and bringing them to God (LS, 62).

FRIDAY

Living holocausts

Surrender is true love. The more we surrender, the more we love God and souls. If we really love souls, we must be ready to take their place, to take their sins upon us and expiate them. We must be living holocausts, for the souls need us as such.

There is no limit to God's love. It is without measure and its depth cannot be sounded. "I will not leave you orphans" (LC, 103).

SATURDAY

To share Christ's suffering

The Church invites us, in response to the unmeasured love of Christ, to fill up in our flesh what is lacking of the suffering of Christ on behalf of His Body, the Church; to express our union and sharing in the sufferings of our poor, for their salvation and sanctification; to give this witness of penance so that the people of God will have the courage to accept it also in their own lives (Const, no. 127).

CARRYING OUR CROSSES

"If any man would come after Me, let him deny himself and take up his cross daily and follow Me" (Lk 9:23).

PASSION SUNDAY

Stations of the Cross

Jesus said to the people of His time, "If you want to be My disciples, take up your cross and come follow Me."

. . . Today in young people of the world, Jesus lives His Passion, in the suffering, in the hungry, the handicapped young people—in that child who eats a piece of bread crumb by crumb, because when that piece of bread is finished, there will be no more and hunger will come again.

That is a Station of the Cross.

Are you there with that child?

And those thousands who die not only for a piece of bread, but for a little bit of love, of recognition. That is a Station of the Cross. Are you there?

And young people, when they fall, as Jesus fell again and again for us, are we there as Simon Cyrene to pick them up, to pick up the Cross?

The people in the parks, the alcoholics, the homeless, they are looking at you. Do not be those who look and do not see.

Look and see.

We can begin the Stations of the Cross step by step with joy. Jesus made Himself the Bread of Life for us.

We have Jesus in the Bread of Life to give us the strength (SV, 282–283).

MONDAY

A carrier of love is a carrier of the cross

Let us not try to escape the cross of humiliations but grab the chance to be like Jesus, to let Him live His Passion in us. A carrier of love means a carrier of the cross. Maybe while carrying the cross we fall. Ask Simon to help you. . . .

On the Cross Jesus showed us the deepest poverty: complete surrender and abandonment to His Father. Today let us put on the poverty of His Passion. Do something today to share in the Passion. Maybe Jesus is asking you something in a special way, maybe something small (Unpub.).

TUESDAY

World's hatred may come to Christ's followers

The following of Christ is inseparable from the Cross of Calvary. "Do you think that I have come to bring peace on earth? No, I tell you, but rather division!" (Mt

10:34). To those who follow Christ fully is given the world's hatred, for they are a challenge to His spirit just as Christ Himself was hated first. Humiliation, lack of appreciation, criticism—we must remember that the people whom He healed or forgave turned round and crucified Him (LS, 61).

WEDNESDAY

What you can see in the Cross

. . . Look at the Cross and you will see Jesus' head bent to kiss you, His arms extended to embrace you, His heart opened to receive you, to enclose you within His love. Knowing that the Cross was His greater love for you and for me, let us accept His Cross in whatever He wants to give, let us give with joy whatever He wants to take, for in doing so they will know that we are His disciples, that we belong to Jesus, that the work you and I and all the Brothers and Sisters do is but our love in action . . . (MTC, 333–334).

MAUNDY THURSDAY

The humility of Jesus

"He began to wash the disciples' feet" (Jn 13:5).
"Take, eat; this is My Body" (Mt 26:26).

Jesus wanted to teach humility. He washed their feet. Meekness. He gave us His Body (Unpub.).

GOOD FRIDAY

The Cross—no greater love . . .

"Crucify Him! Crucify Him!" (Jn 19:6).
"It is finished" (Jn 19:30).

Lord, help us to see in Your crucifixion and Resurrection an example of how to endure and seemingly to die in the agony and conflict of daily life, so that we may live more fully and creatively. You accepted patiently and humbly the rebuffs of human life, as well as the tortures of Your crucifixion and Passion. Help us to accept the pains and conflicts that come to us each day as opportunities to grow as people and become more like You. Enable us to go through them patiently and bravely, trusting that You will support us. Make us realize that it is only by frequent deaths of ourselves and our self-centered desires that we can come to live more fully; for it is only by dying with You that we can rise with You (GG, 73–74).

HOLY SATURDAY

The poverty of Jesus

Our Lord on the Cross possessed nothing. . . . He was
on the Cross that was given by Pilate. The nails and the
crown were given by the soldiers. He was naked and
when He died, Cross, nails and crown were taken away
from Him. He was wrapped in a shroud given by a kind
heart, and buried in a tomb that was not His. Yet Jesus
could have died as a king and He could have risen from
the dead as king. He chose poverty because He knew in
His infinite knowledge and wisdom that it is the real
means of possessing God, of conquering His heart, of
bringing His love down to this earth (LC, 108).

Silence. Be alone with Him in your heart. Our Lady
was silent, even at the Cross (Unpub.).

EASTER

He has risen (Mk 16:6).

Alleluja!

JOY

"Your sorrow will turn into joy" (Jn 16:20).
"Rejoice in the Lord always; again I say, Rejoice" (Phil 4:4).

EASTER SUNDAY

"He has risen" Alleluja!

May the joy of the risen Jesus Christ be with you. To bring joy into our very soul the good God has given Himself to us. In Bethlehem, "joy" said the angel. In His life, He wanted to share His joy with His apostles "that My joy may be in you". Joy was the password of the first Christians. Saint Paul—how often he repeated himself: "Rejoice in the Lord always; and again I say, rejoice" (Phil 4:4). In return for the great grace of baptism the priest tells the newly baptized: "May you serve the Church joyfully." Joy is not simply a matter of temperament in the service of God and souls. It is always hard—all the more reason why we should try to acquire it and make it grow in our hearts (LS, 68).

MONDAY

Joy—a net of love

Joy is prayer; joy is strength; joy is love; joy is a net of love by which you can catch souls (LS, 68).

TUESDAY

Joy cannot be kept closed inside

Joy shows from the eyes; it appears when one speaks and walks. It cannot be kept closed inside us. It reacts outside. When people find in your eyes that habitual happiness, they will understand that they are the beloved children of God. Try to imagine a nun who goes to the slums with a sad face and uncertain step. What would her presence give to those people? Only more depression (LS, 69).

WEDNESDAY

A joyful heart the result of love

Saint Paul says, "Each one must do as he has made up his mind, not reluctantly or under compulsion, for God loves a cheerful giver." He gives most who gives with joy. If in your work you have difficulties and you accept them with joy, with a big smile—in this, as in any other thing, they will see your good works and glorify the Father. The best way to show your gratitude to God and people is to accept everything with joy. A joyful heart is the normal result of a heart burning with love (LS, 68).

THURSDAY

Cheerfulness

Cheerfulness is a sign of a generous person. It is often a cloak that hides a life of sacrifice. A person who has this gift of cheerfulness often reaches great heights of perfection. Let the sick and suffering find us real angels of comfort and consolation. Why has the work in the slums been blessed by God? Not on account of any personal qualities but on account of the joy the Sisters radiate. . . .

Joy is very infectious; therefore, be always full of joy when you go among the poor (LC, 104–105).

FRIDAY

Be in paradise right now

We wait impatiently for the paradise where God is, but we have it in our power to be in paradise with Him, right now; being happy with Him means:
>To love as He loves.
>To help as He helps.
>To give as He gives.
>To serve as He serves (LC, 61–62).

SATURDAY

Be the sunshine of God's love

Today be the sunshine of God's love (Unpub.).

Be happy . . . and make it a special point to become God's sign of happiness in your community. . . . We have to be the "sign of God" of that true poverty of Christ. Therefore, we must radiate the joy of being poor, but do not speak about it. Do not tell people of the hard life—just be happy with Christ (SV, 377).

PEACE

"Peace I leave with you; My peace I give to you" (Jn 14:27).
"Peace be with you" (Jn 20:19).

SECOND SUNDAY OF EASTER

Thank God for His gift of peace

Let us thank God for His gift of peace that reminds us that we have been created to live that peace, and that Jesus became man in all things like us except in sin, and He proclaimed very clearly that He had come to give the Good News. The news was peace to all men of good will and this is something that we all want—peace of heart (LS, 85).

MONDAY

"Let me preach Thee without preaching"

Let us preach the peace of Christ as He did. He went about doing good. He did not stop His works of charity because the Pharisees and others hated Him or tried to spoil His Father's work. He just went about doing good. Cardinal Newman wrote: "Help me to spread Thy fragrance everywhere I go. Let me preach Thee without preaching, not by words but by my example." Our works of love are nothing but the works of peace (LS, 85).

TUESDAY

Peace begins with a smile

Let us not use bombs and guns to overcome the world. Let us use love and compassion. Peace begins with a smile—smile five times a day at someone you don't really want to smile at at all—do it for peace. So let us radiate the peace of God and so light His light and extinguish in the world and in the hearts of all men all hatred and love for power (LS, 85).

WEDNESDAY

If we have no peace . . .

. . . Today if we have no peace it is because we have forgotten that we belong to each other—that man, that woman, that child is my brother or my sister . . . (CW, no. 25).

If everyone could see the image of God in his neighbor, do you think we should still need tanks and generals? (SV, 414).

THURSDAY

The greatest destroyer of peace

Abortion is the killer of peace in the world . . . the greatest destroyer of peace because if a mother can destroy her own child what is left for others but to kill each other? There is nothing to prevent them (RL, 11).

FRIDAY

Nations need to defend the poor

Today, nations put too much effort and money into defending their borders. They know very little about the poverty and the suffering which exist in the countries where those bordering on destitution live. If they would only defend these defenseless people with food, shelter and clothing, I think the world would be a happier place (SMT, 73).

SATURDAY

Work of peace is God's

The poor must know that we love them, that they are wanted. They themselves have nothing to give but love. We are concerned with how to get this message of love and compassion across. We are trying to bring peace to the world through our work. But the work is the gift of God (HP, 139).

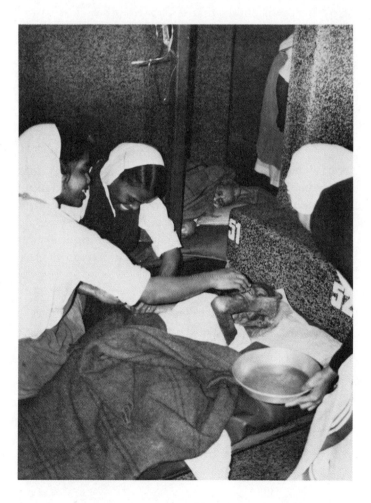

DIVINE PROVIDENCE

"They took so many fish they could not haul the net in" (Jn 21:6).

THIRD SUNDAY OF EASTER

A miracle every day

There is a sort of miracle every day. There is not a day without some delicate attention of God, some sign of His love and care, like the time we ran out of food because of rains and flood. Just that time the schools closed in Calcutta and all the bread was given to us so that the people would not go hungry. For two days, our poor had bread and bread, until they could eat no more. The greatest miracle is that God can work through nothings, small things like us. He uses us to do His work (SV, 266).

MONDAY

How much more will God care for us . . .

. . . Surely if God feeds the young ravens which cry to Him, if He nourishes the birds which neither sow nor reap nor gather into barns; if He vests the flowers of the field so beautifully, how much more will He care for men whom He has made in His own image and likeness and adopted as His children, if we only act as such, keep His commandments and have confidence in Him (LS, 27).

TUESDAY

God faithful to His promises

Our dependence on divine providence is a firm and lively faith that God can and will help us. That He can is evident, because He is almighty; that He will is certain because He promised it in so many passages of Holy Scripture and because He is infinitely faithful to all His promises. Christ encourages us to have this confidence in these words: "Whatever you ask in prayer, believe that you have received it, and it will be yours" (LS, 27).

WEDNESDAY

Not one single day have we refused somebody

If we really fully belong to God, then we must be at His disposal and we must trust in Him. We must never be preoccupied with the future. There is no reason to be so. God is there.

There has not been one single day that we have refused

somebody, that we did not have food, that we did not have a bed or something, and we deal with thousands of people. We have 53,000 lepers and yet never one has been sent away because we did not have. It is always there, though we have no salaries, no income, no nothing, we receive freely and give freely. This has been such a beautiful gift of God . . . (LS, 26).

THURSDAY

Living one day at a time

We should have the joy and freedom of poverty and share the joy of loving.

We are given much, we use much. We live one day at a time relying on divine providence. We experience the joy of the freedom of poverty. We want to feel the joy of sharing. . . . Giving must generate joy (MLP, 33).

FRIDAY

Planned by God

. . . The very fact that God has placed a certain soul in your way is a sign that God wants you to do something for him or her. It is not chance; it has been planned by God. We are bound by conscience to help him or her (LC, 115).

SATURDAY

"Seek ye first the Kingdom of heaven" (Mt 6:33)

. . . The apostle Saint Peter . . . commands us to throw all cares upon the Lord who provides for us. And why should God not care for us since He sent His Son and with Him all? Saint Augustine says: "How can you doubt that God will give you good things since He vouchsafed to assume evil for you?"

This must give us confidence in the providence of God who preserves even the birds and the flowers. . . .

I don't want the work to become a business but to remain a work of love. I want you to have that complete confidence that God won't let us down. Take Him at His word and seek first the Kingdom of heaven, and all else will be added on (LS, 27).

LOVE IN ACTION

"My children, our love is not to be just words or mere talk, but something real and active" (1 Jn 3:18).

FOURTH SUNDAY OF EASTER

Love proved in deeds

Love does not live on words, nor can it be explained by words—especially that love which serves Him, which comes from Him and which finds Him and touches Him. We must reach the heart and to reach the heart as we must do—love is proved in deeds (LS, 40).

MONDAY

Perhaps only a smile

Love of Christ should be a living bond between all of us. Then the world will know that we are true missionaries of charity.

Perhaps only a smile, a little visit, or simply the fact of building a fire for someone, writing a letter for a blind person, bringing a few coals, finding a pair of shoes, reading for someone, this is only a little bit, yes, a very tiny bit, but it will be our love of God in action (LC, 26).

TUESDAY

Not how much we do but how much we love

Never think that a small action done to your neighbor is not worth much. It is not how much we do that is pleasing to God, but how much love we put into the doing. That is what the good God looks for—because He is love and He has made us in His image to love and to be loved.

Make sure you know your neighbor, for that knowledge will lead you to great love and love to personal service (AP, 7).

WEDNESDAY

Ordinary things with extraordinary love

Teach your children to pray and pray with them. Jesus has made Himself the Bread of Life to give us His life, to become like Him; so let us be holy like Jesus, full of compassion, full of humility toward each other; for in loving one another we love Him. How do we love? Not in big things but in small things with great love. When the Little Flower was canonized the Holy Father said: "She did ordinary things with extraordinary love" (S, Rome, October 31, 1982).

THURSDAY

Listening groups

In some places, like in England, we have Co-Workers composing small "listening groups". They go to people, ordinary old people's houses, and sit down with them and let them talk and talk. Very old people love to have somebody listen to them and let them talk and talk. Very old people love to have somebody listen to them even if they have to tell the story of thirty years ago.

To listen, when nobody else wants to listen, is a very beautiful thing (MLP, 74).

FRIDAY

Only small things

We can do no great things—only small things with great love. The Sisters are doing small things: helping the children, visiting the lonely, the sick, the unwanted. In one of the houses the Sisters visited a woman living alone who was dead many days before she was found— and she was found because her body had begun to decompose. The people around her did not even know her name.

When someone told me that the Sisters had not started any big work, that they were quietly doing small things, I said even if they helped one person, that was enough. Jesus would have died for one person, for one sinner (LS, 45).

SATURDAY

The warmth of a human hand

One day I was walking down the streets of London and I saw a man quite drunk. He was looking so sad and miserable I went right up to him and took his hand, shook it and asked, "How are you?" My hand is always warm—and he said, "Oh, after so long I feel the warmth of a human hand." And his face lit up. And his face was different. I only want to say that small things done in great love bring joy and peace (IT, no. 4).

VINE AND BRANCHES

"I am the vine, you are the branches" (Jn 15:5).

FIFTH SUNDAY OF EASTER

Each of us a branch

The fifteenth chapter of Saint John will bring us close to Christ. This chapter of Saint John I think is so fitting for us because the branch on the vine is exactly what every Co-Worker is. The Father, being the gardener, has to prune that branch to be able to bring forth much fruit and the fruit that we have to bring into the world is very beautiful—the love of the Father ("As the Father has loved Me, so I have loved you") and joy ("Abide in Me that My joy may be in you"). Each one of us is a branch (LS, 59).

MONDAY

Vine and branches joined so tightly

When I was last in Rome I wanted to give a little instruction to my novice Sisters and I thought this chapter [John 15] was the most beautiful means of understanding

what we are to Jesus and what Jesus is to us. But I had
not realized as those young Sisters had realized when
they looked at the joining of the vine and branches that
the joining was so tight—as if the vine were afraid that
something or somebody would separate the branch from
it (LS, 59).

TUESDAY

All fruit is on the branches

[Another] thing that the Sisters drew my attention to
was that when they looked at the vine they could see
no fruit. All the fruit was on the branches. Then they
told me that the humility of Jesus is so great that He
needs the branch to produce the fruit. That is why He
has taken so much care over the joining—to be able to
produce that fruit He has made it a joining that somebody
will have to use force to separate (LS, 59–60).

WEDNESDAY

Pruning the branch to bring more fruit

The Father, the gardener, prunes the branch to bring
more fruit and the branch silently, lovingly, uncondi-
tionally, lets itself be pruned. We know what the pruning

is, for in all our lives there must be the cross and the closer we are to Him the greater is the touch of the cross, and the pruning is much more intimate and delicate (LS, 60).

THURSDAY

Become real branches on Jesus' vine

Let us become real branches, filled with fruit, on Jesus' vine. Let us welcome Him into our lives whenever He wants to come in. He comes as Truth which must be spoken, as Life which must be lived, as Light which must be reflected, as Love which must be loved, as the Way which we must take, as Happiness which we must spread, as Peace which we must plant, as Sacrifice which we must offer in our families and with our neighbors—whether near or far (SMT, 37).

FRIDAY

All are witness of Christ

We must all be witnesses of Christ. Christ is the vine and we are the branches. Without us, there would be no fruit. This is something to bear in mind. God is the

vinedresser to all of us. Christ made no distinction between priests and Brothers, Sisters and laywomen, no
distinction as witness-bound. We must all be witnesses
of Christ's compassion, Christ's love, to our families,
to our neighbors, to the towns or cities where we reside,
and to the world in which we live (LC, 16).

SATURDAY

A Co-Worker of Christ

Each one of us is a Co-Worker of Christ, the branch on
that vine, so what does it mean for you and me to be a
Co-Worker of Christ? It means to abide in His love, to
have His joy, to spread His compassion, to be a witness
to His presence in the world (LS, 60).

LOVE ONE ANOTHER

"A new commandment I give to you, that you love one another; even as I have loved you, that you also love one another" (Jn 13:34).

SIXTH SUNDAY OF EASTER

Love as normal as living and breathing

"Love one another, even as I have loved you." These words should be not only a light to us, but also a flame consuming the selfishness which prevents the growth of holiness. Jesus loved us to the end, to the very limit of love, the Cross. Love must come from within—from our union with Christ—an outpouring of our love for God. Loving should be as normal to us as living and breathing, day after day until our death (LS, 37).

MONDAY

Where do we share the joy of loving?

God gives us that great strength and the great joy of loving those He has chosen. Do we use it? Where do we use it first? Jesus said love one another. He didn't say love the world, He said, love one another—right here, my brother, my neighbor, my husband, my wife, my child, the old ones (LS, 38).

TUESDAY

You are a liar

How do we love God? Where is God? We know, we believe He is everywhere. And to make it easy for us to understand this presence, to understand this love, we read again in the Scripture that Saint John says, how, how can you say that you love God whom you don't see if you don't love a neighbor whom you see? And he uses a very big word. "You are a liar." It is a big word. It is one of those words that is frightening to read in the Gospel, and yet it's really true. And where does this love begin? It begins at home (Talk 4).

WEDNESDAY

"My mother does not want me"

Our Sisters are working around the world and I have seen all the trouble, all the misery, all the suffering. From where did it come? It has come from lack of love and lack of prayer. There is no coming together in the family, praying together, coming together, staying together. Love begins at home and we will find the poor even in our own home.

We have a house in London. Our Sisters there work at night and one night they went out to pick up the people on the streets. They saw a young man there late at night, lying in the street, and they said, "You should not be here, you should be with your parents", and he said, "When I go home my mother does not want me because I have long hair. Every time I go home she pushes me out." By the time they came back he had taken an overdose and they had to take him to hospital. I could not help thinking it was quite possible his mother was busy, with the hunger of our people in India, and there was her own child hungry for her, hungry for her love, hungry for her care and she refused it.

It is easy to love the people far away. It is not always easy to love those close to us. It is easier to give a cup of rice to relieve hunger than to relieve the loneliness and pain of someone unloved in our own home. Bring love into your home for this is where our love for each other must start (LS, 38–39).

THURSDAY

(Ascension Day)

"As He blessed them He left them and was taken up to heaven"
(Lk 24:51).

Jesus makes it "easy"

To make it easy for us to really love God, really be holy,
Jesus again and again and again said the same thing:
"Love one another as I have loved you." When we look
at the Cross we know how much He loved us. When
we look at the Tabernacle we know how much He loves
us now. And to make it, again I say, "easy" for us, He
says, "Whatever you do to the least of My brethren,
you do it to Me." "I was hungry; I was naked; I was
homeless . . ." (Talk 4).

FRIDAY

"Love" can be misused

Love can be misused for selfish motives. I love you, but
at the same time I want to take from you as much as I
can, even the things that are not for me to take. Then
there is no true love any more. True love hurts. It always
has to hurt. It must be painful to love someone, painful
to leave them, you might have to die for them. When
people marry they have to give up everything to love

each other. The mother who gives birth to her child suffers much. It is the same in religious life. To belong fully to God we have to give up everything. Only then can we truly love. The word "love" is so misunderstood and so misused (HP, 139–140).

SATURDAY

When will we love one another?

We will love one another when we hear the voice of God in our hearts (Unpub.).

"THAT ALL MAY BE ONE"

". . . that all may be one" (Jn 17:21).

SEVENTH SUNDAY OF EASTER

Remain one

"May they all be one.
Father, may they be one in Us,
as You are in Me and I am in You,
so that the world may believe it was
You who sent Me" (Jn 17:21).

God will take care of you, if you remain one! (SV, 422).

MONDAY

No matter what religion, what matters is that we love

Some call Him Ishwar, some call Him Allah, some simply God, but we all have to acknowledge that it is He who made us for greater things: to love and to be loved. What matters is that we love. We cannot love without prayer, and so whatever religion we are we must pray together (LS, 82).

TUESDAY

We complete each other

It is so beautiful that we complete each other! What we are doing in the slums, maybe you cannot do. What you are doing in the level where you are called—in your family life, in your college life, in your work—we cannot do. But you and we together are doing something beautiful for God (MLP, 41).

WEDNESDAY

God works in His own ways

Every human being comes from the hand of God and we all know what is the love of God for us. My religion is everything to me but for every individual, according to the grace God has given that soul.

God has His own ways and means to work in the hearts of men, and we do not know how close they are to Him, but by their actions we will always know whether they are at His disposal or not. . . . We must not condemn or judge or pass words that will hurt people. Maybe a person has never heard of Christianity. We do not know what way God is appearing to that soul and what way God is drawing that soul, and therefore, who are we to condemn anybody? (LS, 81–82).

THURSDAY

All people the same

There is no great difference in reality between one country and another, because it is always people you meet everywhere. They may look different or be dressed differently, they may have a different education or position; but they are all the same. They are all people to be loved; they are all hungry for love (GG, 53).

The people you see on the streets of India or Hong Kong are hungry in body, but the people in London or New York have also a hunger which must be satisfied. Every person needs to be loved (LS, 82).

FRIDAY

What is a communist?

I was invited last year to China, and one of the Chinese talk people asked, "And what is a communist to you?" And I said, "A child of God, my brother, my sister". And nobody had another word to say. Nobody. Perfect silence. The next day in all the communist papers, "Mother Teresa says, 'A communist is a child of God, my brother, my sister.'" And I didn't tell a lie and it is true, because the same loving hand created you, created me, created that man in the street. And it is there where love must be shown (Talk 4).

SATURDAY

We all work as one

We have absolutely no difficulty regarding having to work in countries with many faiths, like India. We treat all people as children of God. They are our brothers and sisters. We show great respect to them. . . .

Our work is to encourage these Christians and non-Christians to do works of love. And every work of love, done with a full heart, always brings people closer to God.

If they accept God in their lives, then they are a co-worker. If they don't, it's their answer (MLP, 21).

PENTECOST

Come Holy Spirit!

When Pentecost day came around, they had all met in one room, when suddenly they heard what sounded like a powerful wind from heaven, the noise of which filled the entire house in which they were sitting. . . . They were all filled with the Holy Spirit, and began to speak foreign languages as the Spirit gave them the gift of speech (Acts 2:1–4).

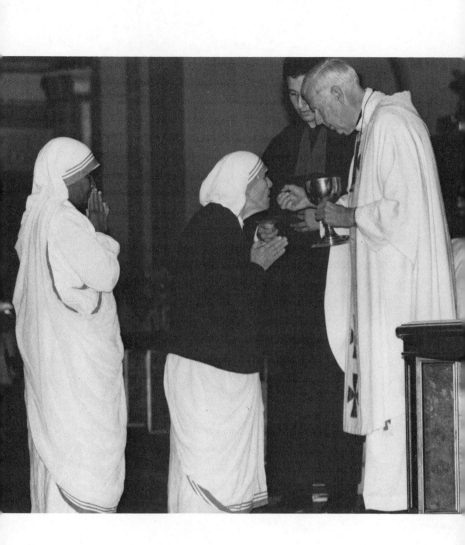

JESUS WITH US

"If anyone thirst, let him come to Me and drink" (Jn 7:37).

THE DAY OF PENTECOST

Jesus comes again and again

The coming of Jesus in Bethlehem brought joy to the
world and every human heart. The same Jesus comes
again and again in our hearts during Holy Communion.
He wants to give the same joy and peace. May His
coming bring to each one of us that peace and joy which
He desires to give. Let us pray much for this grace in
our own hearts, our communities and in the Church
(LS, 69).

MONDAY

Christ with us

Let us keep that joy of loving Jesus in our hearts, and
share that joy with all that we come in touch with. That
radiating joy is real, for we have no reason not to be
happy because we have Christ with us. Christ in our
hearts, Christ in the poor that we meet, Christ in the
smile that we give and the smile we receive . . . (Talk 5).

TUESDAY

Jesus loves us

I think that this is something, that we must live life
beautifully, we have Jesus with us and He loves us. If
we could only remember that God loves us, and we
have an opportunity to love others as He loves us, not
in big things, but in small things with great love . . .
(Talk 5).

WEDNESDAY

Without Him we could do nothing

Without Him we could do nothing. And it is at the altar
that we meet our suffering poor. And in Him that we
see that suffering can become a means to greater love
and greater generosity (GG, 20).

THURSDAY

Jesus to me

This is Jesus to me:
The Word made flesh.
The Bread of life.
The Victim offered for our sins on the Cross.
The Sacrifice offered at the Holy Mass for the sins of
the world and mine.
The Word—to be spoken.
The Truth—to be told.
The Way—to be walked.
The Light—to be lit.
The Life—to be lived.
The Love—to be loved.
The Joy—to be shared.
The Sacrifice—to be offered.
The Peace—to be given.
The Bread of Life—to be eaten.
The Hungry—to be fed.
The Thirsty—to be satiated.
The Naked—to be clothed.
The Homeless—to be taken in.
The Sick—to be healed.
The Lonely—to be loved.
The Unwanted—to be wanted.
The Leper—to wash his wounds.
The Beggar—to give him a smile.
The Drunkard—to listen to him.
The Mental—to protect him.
The Little One—to embrace him.

The Blind—to lead him.
The Dumb—to speak for him.
The Crippled—to walk with him.
The Drug Addict—to befriend him.
The Prostitute—to remove from danger and befriend her.
The Prisoner—to be visited.
The Old—to be served.

To me Jesus is my God.
  Jesus is my Spouse.
  Jesus is my Life.
  Jesus is my only Love.
  Jesus is my All in all.
  Jesus is my Everything. (MLP, 106–107).

FRIDAY

He gives you, to share

Open your hearts to the love of God which He will give you—He loves you with tenderness. And He will give you, not to keep, but to share (CW, no. 26).

Jesus, I believe in Your tender love for me. I love You (Unpub.).

SATURDAY

He is always speaking

Why did God choose you? He wants you to be real
missionaries. Look at this great gift of God to you. Listen
to the voice of God. He is always speaking to us. He
wants from us deep love, compassion and forgiveness
(CW, no. 29).

THE VISITATION

(May 31)

The unborn child proclaims Jesus

*"And it came to pass, that when Elisabeth heard the salutation
of Mary, the babe leaped in her womb; and Elisabeth was
filled with the Holy Ghost: And she spake out with a loud
voice, and said, 'Blessed art thou among women, and blessed
is the fruit of thy womb'"* (Lk 1:41–42).

We read in the Scripture that God loved the world so
much that He gave His Son Jesus who became small,
helpless in the womb of His Mother. He was like us in
all things except sin. And on coming to His Mother—His
Mother, having the presence of Jesus Himself in her
womb—she went in haste to serve others. The fruit of
the coming of Jesus is always the need to give Him to

others. And she went to serve her cousin who was also with a child.

And something very beautiful, something very wonderful happened at their meeting. The first one, first human being to recognize the presence of the coming of Jesus, the Son of God, . . . the little one in the womb of his mother, leaped with joy. He recognized that He had come. And it's so beautiful to think that God gave that little unborn child the greatness of proclaiming the presence of God, the presence of Jesus on earth (Talk 2).

GOD'S LOVE

"For God so loved the world that He gave His only Son, that whoever believes in Him should not perish but have eternal life" (Jn 3:16).

FIRST SUNDAY AFTER PENTECOST
(Trinity Sunday)

The Good News

The Good News is that God still loves the world through you. You are God's Good News. You are God's love in action. Each time anyone comes in contact with us, they must become different and better people because of having met us. We must radiate God's love (Unpub.).

MONDAY

He chose to become a creature

He who is "God from God, Light from Light, begotten not made" chose to become a creature for love of us (Unpub.).

TUESDAY

Jesus there to teach love

There will always be misunderstandings; words will be said. There will always be somebody to carry tales, but Jesus is there to teach us how to love (Unpub.).

WEDNESDAY

The tenderness of God's love

I want you to realize the tenderness of God's love:

> I have called you by your name.
> You are Mine.
> Water of temptation will not drown you.
> Fire of sin will not burn you.
> I have carved you in the palm of My hand.
> You are precious to Me.
> I love you (from Is 43).

Keep the joy of loving God, loving Jesus in your heart, and share that joy with all you meet (Talk 3).

THURSDAY

Natural to radiate His love

A Christian is a tabernacle of the living God. He created me; He chose me; He came to dwell in me, because He wanted me. Now that you have known how much God is in love with you, it is but natural that you spend the rest of your life radiating that love (GG, 30).

FRIDAY

An infinitely faithful love

Be not afraid. God loves you and wants us to love one another as He loves us. As miserable, weak and shameful as we are, He loves us with an infinitely faithful love (IN, 67).

SATURDAY

Love grows from our union with Christ

It is very difficult to give Jesus to the people unless we have Jesus in our hearts.

We all should become the carriers of God's love. But to do this, we must deepen our life of love and prayer and sacrifice.

We must bring peace, love and compassion to the world today. We don't need guns and bombs to do this. We need deep love, deep union with Christ to be able to give Him to others.

Compassion and love have to grow from within, from our union with Christ. And from that union, love for the family, love for the neighbor, love for the poor is a natural fruit (MLP, 100).

THE BODY OF CHRIST

"And as they were eating, He took bread, and blessed, and broke it, and gave it to them, and said, 'Take; this is My Body'" (Mk 14:22).

SECOND SUNDAY AFTER PENTECOST
(Corpus Christi)

Jesus: the Living Bread, understanding love

The meaning of this Eucharist is understanding love. Christ understood. He understood that we have a terrible hunger for God. He understood that we have been created to be loved, and so He made Himself a Bread of Life and He said, "Unless you eat My flesh and drink My blood, you cannot live, you cannot love, you cannot serve." You must eat this Bread and the goodness of the love of Christ to share His understanding love.

He also wants to give us the chance to put our love for Him in a living action. He makes Himself the hungry one, not only for bread, but for love. He makes Himself the naked one, not only for a piece of cloth but for that understanding love, that dignity, human dignity. He makes Himself the homeless one, not only for the piece of a small room, but for that deep sincere love for the other, and this is the Eucharist. This is Jesus, the Living Bread that He has come to break with you and me (MTC, 163–164).

MONDAY

The Eucharist, our glory and joy

Holy Mass is the prayer of our day where we offer ourselves with Christ to be broken and given to the poorest of the poor.

The Eucharist is our glory and joy and the mystery of our union with Christ (Unpub.).

TUESDAY

"Mother, I have been touching the body of Christ"

A girl came from outside India to join the Missionaries of Charity. We have a rule that the very next day new arrivals must go to the Home for the Dying. So I told this girl: "You saw Father during Holy Mass, with what love and care he touched Jesus in the Host. Do the same when you go to the Home for the Dying, because it is the same Jesus you will find there in the broken bodies of our poor."

And they went. After three hours the newcomer came back and said to me with a big smile—I have never seen a smile quite like that—"Mother, I have been touching the body of Christ for three hours." And I said to her: "How—what did you do?" She replied: "When we arrived there, they brought a man who had fallen into a drain, and been there for some time. He was covered

with wounds and dirt and maggots, and I cleaned him
and I knew I was touching the body of Christ" (GG,
56–57).

WEDNESDAY

We must have Jesus to give Him to others

The Church . . . has entrusted us with the great apostolate to bring Christ into the hearts of our people. We
must give Jesus to them. But unless we have Jesus, we
cannot give Him. That is why we need the Eucharist.
It is true, our way of life is difficult. It has to be like
that. It is not only the material poverty, but the poverty
of being surrounded by suffering people, by death. Only
the Eucharist, only Jesus, can give us the joy of doing
the work with a smile (SV, 263).

THURSDAY

The food that sustains me

The Mass is the spiritual food that sustains me, without
which I could not get through one single day or hour
in my life; in the Mass we have Jesus in the appearance
of bread, while in the slums we see Christ and touch
Him in the broken bodies, in the abandoned children
(GG, 76).

FRIDAY

When we recollect . . .

When we recollect that in the morning we have held in our hands an all-holy God, we are more ready to abstain from whatever could soil their purity. Hence we should have deep reverence for our own person and reverence for others, treat all with accepted marks of courtesy, but abstain from sentimental feeling or ill-ordered affections. When we handle the sick and the needy we touch the suffering body of Christ and this touch will make us heroic; it will make us forget the repugnance (LC, 109).

SATURDAY

So small, so fragile, so helpless

The world is hungry for God and when Jesus came into the world He wanted to satisfy that hunger. He made Himself the Bread of Life, so small, so fragile, so helpless, and as if that was not enough, He made Himself the hungry one, the naked one, the homeless one, so that we can satisfy His hunger for love—for our human love, not something extraordinary but our human love (LS, 35).

LESSONS FROM OUR LADY

"Mary arose and went with haste . . ." (Lk 1:39).

THIRD SUNDAY AFTER PENTECOST

Sharing what she received

Our Lady, . . . the most beautiful of all women, the greatest, the humblest, the most pure, the most holy, the moment she felt she was full of grace, full of Jesus, went in haste—and here she is a model for all women—by sharing immediately what she had received. This is, so to say, like the breaking of the Eucharist; and we know what happened to Saint John the Baptist; he leaped with joy at the presence of Christ (MTC, 196).

MONDAY

Mary, the first altar

"God loved the world so much that He gave His only Son" (Jn 3:16) and I think that was the first Eucharist, the giving of the Son whom God gave to Our Lady, and Our Lady was the first altar, and she was the one who can in all sincerity say, "This is my body." For she gave her body, her strength, her whole being in making the body of Christ. In her the power of the Holy Spirit dwelled and the Word was made flesh, and she in turn in surrendering herself in total surrender to the living God, when this coming of Christ was announced to her through the angel, asked only one question.

She had offered her virginity, her chastity, her purity to God; and had to keep her promise; but when the angel explained how it would be, she answered with the beautiful words: "I am the handmaid of the Lord, let it be done unto me according to your word" (Lk 1:38) (MTC, 195–196).

TUESDAY

Silence, kindness, humility

Mary can teach us silence—how to keep all things in our hearts as she did, to pray in the silence of our hearts.

Mary can teach us kindness—she went in haste to serve Elizabeth. "They have no wine", she told Jesus at Cana. Let us, like her, be aware of the needs of the poor, be they spiritual or material and let us, like her, give generously of the love and grace we are granted.

Mary will teach us humility—though full of grace yet only the handmaid of the Lord, she stands as one of us at the foot of the Cross, a sinner needing redemption. Let us, like her, touch the dying, the poor, the lonely and the unwanted according to the graces we have received and let us not be ashamed or slow to do the humble work (LS, 22–23).

WEDNESDAY

Nothingness

Take your eyes away from yourself and rejoice that you have nothing, are nothing, can do nothing. Give Jesus a big smile each time your nothingness frightens you. Cling to Our Lady, for she too, before she could become full of grace, full of Jesus, had to go through that darkness (Unpub.).

THURSDAY

Make our hearts meek and humble

Let us ask Our Lady to make our hearts "meek and humble" as her Son's was. It is so very easy to be proud and harsh and selfish—so easy; but we have been created for greater things. How much we can learn from Our Lady! She was so humble because she was all for God. She was full of grace (GG, 49).

FRIDAY

Carrying God's love

A Missionary of Charity is a carrier of God's love. At the Annunciation as soon as Our Lady had received Jesus she went in haste to give Him to others. We must have Jesus in our hearts if we want to become true Co-Workers of Christ. We have to receive Jesus, we have to receive His love, His compassion, and we have to be in haste to give Him to others. If that is not our concern, then we are wasting time. Just doing work is no reason at all, but our reason is to bring peace, love and compassion to the world today. We need that deep love, that deep union with Christ, to be able to give Him to others (MTC, 332).

SATURDAY

Continual trusting

Our Lady had to declare that she was the handmaid of the Lord before God could fill her. Even seeing Jesus die, Our Lady trusted God. . . . Our Lady became the Mother of Sorrows because she said yes continually with full trust and joy, trusting in Him without reserve (Unpub.).

LIFE OF POVERTY

"Foxes have holes, and birds of the air have nests; but the Son of Man has nowhere to lay His head" (Lk 9:58).

FOURTH SUNDAY AFTER PENTECOST

We must be poor to serve and understand the poor

The poor show faith and patience in suffering, . . . and we are privileged to serve God in them. We can console Christ in His distressing disguise in them, Christ suffering in His brethren. . . .

To serve well our poor, we must understand them; to understand their poverty, we must experience it. Working for them, we come to identify ourselves with them. Our Sisters must feel as they feel, feel their poverty before God, know what it is to live without security, depending on God for the morrow (MTC, 221).

MONDAY

The poverty of the poor is so hard

God wants me to be a lonely nun, laden with the poverty of the Cross. Today I learned a good lesson. The poverty of the poor is so hard. When I was going and going till my legs and arms were paining, I was thinking how they have to suffer to get food and shelter. Then the comfort of Loreto came to tempt me, but of my own free choice, my God, and out of love for You, I desire to remain and do whatever is Your holy will in my regard. Give me courage now, this moment.

(From a record kept by Mother Teresa of early days, written at the request of Archbishop Perier [SV, 38].)

TUESDAY

Belonging nowhere

When Jesus talks about hunger He not only refers to physical hunger but to a hunger for love, for understanding, for warmth. He certainly experienced a lack of affection—He came among His own and was rejected. He knew the meaning of loneliness, rejection and of "belonging nowhere". This kind of hunger is very prevalent in our world today; and it is destroying many lives, many homes and many countries. Being dispossessed refers not only to not having a roof over our head but also to not having someone who understands us and is kind to us. This kind of deprivation cries out for someone to open up his or her heart and to take in the lonely, who have no family or human affection of any kind (SMT, 51).

WEDNESDAY

How much we owe the poor

Our life of poverty is as necessary as the work itself. Only in heaven will we see how much we owe to the poor for helping us to love God better because of them (GG, 35).

THURSDAY

I want to stay with the poorest of the poor

O God, through free choice and through Your love, I want to stay here and do Your will. No, I cannot go back. My community are the poor. Their security is mine. Their health is my health. My home is the home of the poor: not just of the poor, but of those who are the poorest of the poor. Of those to whom one tries not to get too close for fear of catching something, for fear of the dirt, or because they are covered in germs and disease. Of those that do not go to pray because they can't leave their houses naked. Of those that no longer eat because they haven't the strength. Of those that fall in the streets, knowing that they are going to die, while the living walk by their sides ignoring them. Of those who no longer cry, because they have no tears left. Of the untouchables (MLP, 10).

FRIDAY

Life of poverty as necessary as the work

We receive everything free, we give everything free, purely for the love of God.

Our life of poverty is as necessary as the work itself.

God always provides. He will always provide. Though we have no income, no salary, no grants, no church maintenance, yet we have never had to send anybody away because we didn't have.

I have never been in need, but I accept what people give for the poor. I need nothing for myself. I never refuse what people give (MLP, 51).

SATURDAY

Keep poverty; poverty makes us free

If you (my Sisters) ever have to get things, you must buy things of cheaper quality. We must be proud of being poor. . . . If you have to sleep in a corner where there is no breeze, do not gasp and pant to show how much you feel it. In these little things one can practice poverty. Poverty makes us free. That is why we can joke and smile and keep a happy heart for Jesus. . . .

Keep to the simple ways of poverty, of repairing your own shoes, and so forth, in short, of loving poverty as you love your mother. Our Society will live as long as that real poverty exists. The institutes where poverty is faithfully practiced are fervent and need not fear decay. We must always try to be poorer still and discover new ways to live our vows of poverty.

. . . We must not spend time and energy on the house by making it look attractive and beautiful. God save us from such convents where the poor would be afraid to enter lest their misery be a cause of shame to them.

. . . Sisters shall live by begging alms. We depend entirely on the charity of the people. The Sisters should not be ashamed to beg from door to door if necessary. Our Lord Himself has promised a reward even for a cup of water given in His name. It is for His sake that we become beggars (LC, 106–108).

PURE HEART

"Blessed are the pure in heart, for they shall see God" (Mt 5:8).

FIFTH SUNDAY AFTER PENTECOST

A pure heart can see God

But to be able to see the face of God you need a clean heart, a heart full of love, and you can only have a heart full of love if it is completely pure, clean and free; and as long as we in our own hearts are not able to hear that voice, the voice of God when He speaks in the silence of our hearts, we will not be able to pray, we will not be able to express our love in action . . . (CW, 25).

MONDAY

To love God without obstacles

God dwells in us. That's what gives Him a beautiful power. It doesn't matter where you are as long as you are clean of heart. He is there with you and within you twenty-four hours. That's why He says, "Love others like I love you." Clean of heart means openness, that complete freedom, that detachment that allows you to love God without hindrance, without obstacles. When sin comes into our life that is a personal obstacle between me and God. He cannot act through me or give me strength when there is sin between us. Sin is nothing but slavery (HP, 145–146).

TUESDAY

Prayer gives a clean heart

Prayer will give you a clean heart, and a clean heart will be able to see God. And if you see God in each other, you will love one another (Talk 3).

WEDNESDAY

Free our minds

Let us free our minds from all that is not Jesus (Unpub.).

THURSDAY

Go to the altar with a pure heart

Bitterness and pride are twin sisters—moodiness goes with them. . . . Do not go to the altar of God with them in your heart. Go with a pure heart. A pure heart will see God (Unpub.).

FRIDAY

Seek God everywhere

Seek always the beauty and goodness of God everywhere (Unpub.).

SATURDAY

Ask Our Lady for help

. . . So let us ask Our Lady to help us to keep our hearts pure so that we can love Christ, her Son, with tenderness and love. . . .

Let us ask Our Lady, in a very special way: Mary, mother of Jesus, be a Mother to each of us, that we, like you, may be pure in heart, that we, like you, love Jesus; that we, like you, serve the poorest, for we are all poor . . . (CW, 26).

"KNOW THYSELF"

"Examine yourselves, to see whether you are holding to your faith. Test yourselves. Do you not realize that Jesus Christ is in you?" (2 Cor 13:5).

SIXTH SUNDAY AFTER PENTECOST

Self-knowledge gives humility

Self-knowledge puts us on our knees, and it is very necessary for love. For knowledge of God gives love, and knowledge of self gives humility (LC, 113).

MONDAY

What have we that we have not received?

Humility is nothing but truth. "What have we got that we have not received?" asks Saint Paul. If I have received everything, what good have I of my own? If we are convinced of this we will never raise our head in pride. If you are humble nothing will touch you, neither praise nor disgrace, because you know what you are. If you are blamed you will not be discouraged. If they call you a saint you will not put yourself on a pedestal (LS, 50).

TUESDAY

Plenty of good and plenty of bad

Saint Augustine says: "Fill yourselves first and then only will you be able to give to others." Self-knowledge is very necessary for confession. That is why the saints could say they were wicked criminals. They saw God and then saw themselves—and they saw the difference. Hence they were not surprised when anyone accused them, even falsely. . . . Each one of you has plenty of good as well as plenty of bad in her. Let none glory in her success but refer all to God (LC, 113).

WEDNESDAY

Work without love is useless

We must never think any one of us is indispensable. God has His ways and means. He may allow everything to go upside down in the hands of a very talented and capable Sister. God sees only her love. She may exhaust herself, even kill herself with work, but unless her work is interwoven with love it is useless. God does not need her work. God will not ask that Sister how many books she has read, how many miracles she has worked, but He will ask her if she has done her best, for the love of Him . . . (LC, 113–114).

THURSDAY

A danger to forget we are sinners

The danger for us is to forget that we are sinners (LC, 112).

FRIDAY

Hold your tongue

. . . We have grown so used to each other that some think they are free to say anything to anybody at any time. They expect the Sisters to bear with their unkindness. Why not try first to hold your tongue? You know what you can do, but you do not know how much the other can bear (LC, 114).

SATURDAY

Examination of conscience a partnership

The first lesson of the heart of Jesus is our examination of conscience. "Know thyself." Examen is a partnership between us and Jesus. We should not rest in useless looks at our own miseries, but should lift our hearts to God and His light . . . (LC, 76).

BEING SENT

"And He called to Him the Twelve, and began to send them out two by two . . ." (Mk 6:7).

SEVENTH SUNDAY AFTER PENTECOST

A person who is sent

Ours is a mission of love. We are there to bring Christ to the people and to bring the people to Christ.

A Missionary of Charity is a person who is sent. Being Missionaries of Charity, we are sent to bring God's love, to prove God's love: that God loves the world, that God loves the poor. He shows His love through us for them (MLP, 17–18).

MONDAY

Proclaiming is not preaching

We must proclaim Christ by the way we talk, by the way we walk, the way we laugh, by our life, so that everyone will know that we belong to Him.

Proclaiming is not preaching; it is being (SV, 330).

TUESDAY

One at a time

What we do is nothing but a drop in the ocean. But if we didn't do it, the ocean would be one drop less.

We have no reason to be despondent or discouraged or unhappy, because we are doing it to Jesus.

I know there are thousands and thousands of poor, but I think of only one at a time.

Jesus was only one and I take Jesus at His word. He has said, "You did it to Me. . . ."

My Sisters, the Brothers and I, we take one person, one individual person, at a time.

You can save only one at a time. We can love only one at a time (MLP, 20).

WEDNESDAY

We must not be afraid

A missionary is a carrier of God's love, a burning light that gives light to all; the salt of the earth. It is said of Saint Francis Xavier that he "stood up as a fire, and his words burnt like a torch". We have to carry Our Lord in places where He has not walked before. The Sisters must be consumed with one desire: Jesus. We must not be afraid to do the things He did—to go fearlessly through death and danger with Him and for Him (LC, 101).

THURSDAY

Raise funds of love

Let us more and more insist on raising funds of love, of kindness, of understanding, of peace. Money will come if we seek first the Kingdom of God; the rest will be given (GG, 33–34).

FRIDAY

Be an angel of comfort

As each Sister is to become a Co-Worker of Christ in the slums, each ought to understand what God and the Missionaries of Charity expect from her. Let Christ radiate and live His life in her and through her in the slums. Let the poor, seeing her, be drawn to Christ and invite Him to enter their homes and their lives. Let the sick and suffering find in her a real angel of comfort and consolation. Let the little ones of the streets cling to her because she reminds them of Him, the friend of the little ones (GG, 34–35).

SATURDAY

We do not wait for numbers

I do not agree with the big way of doing things. To us what matters is an individual. To get to love the person we must come in close contact with him. If we wait till we get the numbers, then we will be lost in the numbers. And we will never be able to show that love and respect for the person. I believe in person to person; every person is Christ for me, and since there is only one Jesus, that person is the only one person in the world for me at that moment (SB, 118).

MARTHA AND MARY

"Now as they went on their way, He entered a village; and a woman named Martha received Him into her house. And she had a sister called Mary, who sat at the Lord's feet and listened to His teaching. But Martha was distracted with much serving; and she went to Him and said, 'Lord, do You not care that my sister has left me to serve alone? Tell her then to help me.' But the Lord answered her, 'Martha, Martha, you are anxious and troubled about many things; one thing is needful. Mary has chosen the good portion, which shall not be taken away from her'" (Lk 10:38–42).

EIGHTH SUNDAY AFTER PENTECOST

To abide in Christ

The life of the soul is the life of Jesus Christ Himself. Jesus with the Father and the Holy Spirit is the efficient cause of sanctifying grace in our souls. By this life, Jesus Christ imparts to me His Spirit. He becomes the principle of a higher activity which prompts me, if I do not put any obstacle in the way, to think, judge, love, suffer and work with Him, by Him and like Him. So our exterior actions become the manifestations of that life of Jesus in me, and I realize the ideal of Saint Paul: "Nevertheless I live, yet not I, but Christ liveth in me." If we learn this interior life, the words of Our Lord will be fulfilled in our regard: "He that abideth in Me, and I in him, the same bringeth forth much fruit" (LS, 30).

MONDAY

Wishing we were doing something else

If you really belong to the work that has been entrusted to you, then you must do it with your whole heart. And you can bring salvation only by being honest and by really working with God. It is not how much we are doing but how much love, how much honesty, how much faith, is put into doing it. It makes no difference what we are doing. What you are doing, I cannot do, and what I am doing, you cannot do. But all of us are doing what God has given us to do. Only sometimes we forget and we spend more time looking at somebody else and wishing we were doing something else (HP, 138).

TUESDAY

Be full of Christ

Our lives to be fruitful must be full of Christ. To be able to bring His peace, joy and love we must have it ourselves for we cannot give what we have not got, like the blind leading the blind (LS, 31).

WEDNESDAY

See only Jesus

Look up and see only Jesus (Unpub.).

THURSDAY

Everybody in a rush

Today we have no time even to look at each other, to talk to each other, to enjoy each other. . . . And so less and less we are in touch with each other. The world is lost for want of sweetness and kindness. People are starving for love because everybody is in such a great rush (LS, 75).

FRIDAY

God surrounds and encompasses you

"I kept the Lord ever before my eyes because He is ever at my right hand that I may not slip", says the Psalmist. God is within me with a more intimate presence than that whereby I am in myself: in Him we live and move and have our being. It is He who gives life to all, that gives power and being to all that exists. But for His sustaining presence, all things would cease to be and fall back into nothingness. Consider that you are in God, surrounded and encompassed by God, swimming in God (LS, 30).

SATURDAY

"Wasting" our life

There may be times when we appear to be wasting our precious life and burying our talents. Our lives are utterly wasted if we use only the light of reason. Our life has no meaning unless we look at Christ . . . (LS, 49).

KNOWING JESUS:
KNOWING THE POOR

" 'Is not this the carpenter, son of Mary and brother of James and Joses and Judas and Simon, and are not His sisters here with us?' And they took offense at Him. And Jesus said to them, 'A prophet is not without honor, except in his own country, and among his own kin, and in his own house.' And He could do no mighty work there, except that He laid His hands upon a few sick people and healed them. And He marveled because of their unbelief" (Mk 6:3–6).

NINTH SUNDAY AFTER PENTECOST

The sadness of Christ

When I see how the poor remain neglected and unrecognized all around us, I understand the sadness of Christ at not being accepted by His own. Today those who ignore or reject the poor, ignore or reject Christ.

The poor do us the honor of allowing us to serve them (MLP, 96).

MONDAY

First know the poor

To serve the poor we must love them. In order to love the poor, we must first know them. And to know them means to know God. Then we must live with the poor; and to live with them means to live with God. Lastly, we must give our hearts in order to love them, and our hands to serve them, and this means to love God and serve Him.

But everything starts from prayer. Without asking God for love, we cannot possess love and still less are we able to give it to others (MTC, 221).

TUESDAY

We serve God in the poor

We must have the conviction that in serving the poor we serve God. God is love. He loves you and me. If we love others as He loves us, it becomes evident that Christ is in the poor and lonely. The certainty of this reality is boundless for me (MTC, 221).

WEDNESDAY

Known only by a room number

Here in England, and in many other places such as Calcutta, we find lonely people who are known only by their addresses, by the number of their room. Where are we, then? Do we really know that there are such people?

These are the people we must know. This is Jesus yesterday and today and tomorrow, and you and I must know who they are. That knowledge will lead us to love them. And that love, to service. Let us not be satisfied with just paying money. Money is not enough. Money can be got. They need your hand to serve them. They need your hearts to love them (SV, 220).

THURSDAY

To restore dignity

[In Tokyo] You are a rich nation, . . . but on one of your streets I saw a man lying drunk, and no one seemed to bother about him, no one tried to restore to him his human dignity, to bring back to his senses a brother, a child of God (MTC, 228).

FRIDAY

The most distressing disguise

How could we turn away from Jesus? Each one is Jesus, only Jesus in a distressing disguise.

Sometimes we meet Jesus rejected and covered in filth in the gutter. Sometimes we find Jesus stuffed into a drain, or moaning with pain of sores or rotting with gangrene—or even screaming from the agony of a broken back. The most distressing disguise calls for even more love from us (SN, 163).

SATURDAY

First see Christ in the poor

If we want the poor to see Christ in us, we must first see Christ in the poor (Unpub.).

MONEY

"There was once a rich man who, having had a good harvest from his land, thought to himself, 'What am I to do? I have not enough room to store my crops.' Then he said, 'This is what I will do: I will pull down my barns and build bigger ones, and store all my grain and my goods in them, and I will say to my soul: My soul, you have plenty of good things laid by for many years to come; take things easy, eat, drink, have a good time.' But God said to him, 'Fool! this very night the demand will be made for your soul; and this hoard of yours, whose will it be then?' So it is when a man stores up treasure for himself in place of making himself rich in the sight of God" (Lk 12:16–21).

TENTH SUNDAY AFTER PENTECOST

What would one do with surplus money?

One loses touch with God when one takes hold of money. God preserve us. It is better to die. What would one do with surplus money? Bank it? We must never get into the habit of being preoccupied with the future. There is no reason to do so: God is there. Once the longing for money comes, the longing also comes for what money can give: superfluous things, nice rooms, luxuries at the table, more clothes, fans and so on. Our needs will increase, for one thing leads to another, and the result will be endless dissatisfaction (LC, 106).

MONDAY

Do not let money make you forget

Do not let money so preoccupy you as to forget that we and our people are more important to God than all the lilies of the field and the birds of the air. Therefore, try more and more to understand that yours is a way of life—the way of Jesus—that will lead you to the perfect love of God and your neighbors. That is holiness. For holiness is not the luxury of the few, but it is a simple duty for you and for me (AP, 7–8).

TUESDAY

Suffocated by things

Here in America, . . . you can easily be suffocated by things. And once you have them you must give time to taking care of them. Then you have no time for each other or for the poor. You must give freely to the poor what the rich get for their money (SV, 328).

WEDNESDAY

Love, the only remedy for some things

Money can only buy material things like food, clothing and shelter. Something else is needed. There are evils that can't be remedied with money . . . only with love . . . (MTC, 19–20).

Money is useful only if it serves to spread Christ's love. It can serve to feed the hungry Christ. But he is hungry not just for bread, but for love, for your presence, for your human contact (SMT, 61).

THURSDAY

Not a sin to be rich

It is not a sin to be rich. There must be a reason why some people can afford to live well. They must have worked for it. But I tell you this provokes avarice, and there comes sin. Richness is given by God and it is our duty to divide it with those less favored (LS, 53).

Who are we that we can judge the rich? Our task is to bring the rich and the poor together, to be their point of contact (LC, 50).

FRIDAY

Angry at wasted resources

("Are you ever angry?" one reporter asked her. "Are you ever frustrated?")

Yes, . . . I get angry sometimes when I see waste, when the things that are wasted are what people need, things that could save them from dying. Frustrated? No, never (SV, 266).

SATURDAY

Will God become bankrupt in New York?

I don't want the work to become a business but to remain a work of love. I want you to have that complete confidence that God won't let us down. Take Him at His word and seek first the Kingdom of heaven, and all else will be added on. Joy, peace and unity are more important than money. If God wants me to do something, He gives me the money. I refused an offer from Cardinal Cooke of five hundred dollars a month for each Sister working in Harlem. I said to him: "Do you think, Your Eminence, that God is going to become bankrupt in New York?" . . . Money—I don't think about it. It always comes. The Lord sends it. We do His work. He provides the means. If He does not give us the means, that shows that He does not want the work so why worry? (ML, 85–86).

SMILE

"A glad heart makes a cheerful countenance" (Prov 15:13).

ELEVENTH SUNDAY AFTER PENTECOST

Smile, the beginning of love

Let us always meet each other with a smile, . . . for a smile is the beginning of love (P, 61).

MONDAY

The good a simple smile can do

We shall never know all the good that a simple smile can do.

We speak of our God, good, clement and understanding; but are we the living proof of it? Those who suffer, can they see this goodness, this forgiving God, this real understanding in us?

Never let anyone come to you without coming away better and happier. Everyone should see goodness in your face, in your eyes, in your smile (LC, 34).

TUESDAY

Smile when Jesus demands much

Jesus can demand a great deal from us. It is precisely in those instances when He demands a great deal from us that we should give Him a beautiful smile (SMT, 63).

WEDNESDAY

Accept and give with a smile

When a poor person comes to you, receive him or her with a smile. This is the greatest gift God has given you: having the strength to accept anything He might give you and being willing to give back to Him anything He might ask of you (AP, 105).

THURSDAY

"Are you married, Mother Teresa?"

Some time ago a big group of professors from the United States came to our house in Calcutta. Before leaving, they said to me, "Tell us something that will help us, that will help us become holy."

And I said to them, "Smile at each other." (Because we have no time even to look at each other.)

And one of them asked me, "Are you married, Mother Teresa?"

I said, "Yes, and I find it sometimes very difficult to smile at Jesus for He can be very demanding" (MLP, 82).

FRIDAY

Smile at one another

Smile at one another. It is not always easy. Sometimes I find it hard to smile at my Sisters, but then we must pray. Prayer begins at home and a family that prays together, stays together. We must give Jesus a home in our homes for only then can we give Him to others (LS, 73).

SATURDAY

Give your heart

. . . To children, to the poor, to all who suffer and are lonely, give always a happy smile. Give them not only your care but also your heart. Because of God's goodness and love every moment of our life can be the beginning of great things (LS, 42).

MARY OUR MOTHER

"Then He said to the disciple, 'Behold, your Mother!'" (Jn 19:27).

TWELFTH SUNDAY AFTER PENTECOST

Mary nourishes life of Christ in us

Mary, under her Divine Son, has sovereign dominion in the administration of supernatural graces and benefits of God's Kingdom. She is our Mother because in her love she cooperated in our spiritual rebirth. She continues to be our Mother by nourishing the life of Christ in us (LC, 100).

MONDAY

(or Assumption, August 15)

A spotless mirror of God's love

Today will be one of the most beautiful feasts of Our Lady. She fulfills her role as cause of our joy. Do we really know why we love Our Lady so much? Because she was the spotless mirror of God's love . . . (LC, 79).

TUESDAY

What a long Holy Communion!

I wish you the joy of Our Lady, who because she was humble of heart could hold Jesus for nine months in her bosom. What a long Holy Communion! (LC, 94).

WEDNESDAY

Love for Our Lady

During this month ask from the Sacred Heart one very special grace—love for Our Lady. Ask Him to help you love her as He loved her . . . and be a cause of joy to her as He was. Share everything with Mary, even the cross—as Jesus did (Unpub.).

THURSDAY

Full of zeal to give Jesus to others

Like Mary, let us be full of zeal to go in haste to give Jesus to others. Like her, we too become full of grace every time we receive Jesus in Holy Communion (Unpub.).

FRIDAY

"Be a Mother to me now"

Keep Mary very close to you, very close. . . .

Two poor people came to our house and they said: "We are married sixteen years, and we have no children. We are longing to have a baby. Will you pray for us, do something?" So I gave them a miraculous medal. They were both Hindu, but I gave miraculous medal, and I told them: "Say often during the day: 'Mary, the Mother of Jesus, give us a baby.'"

And they prayed. And they prayed. They must have prayed God knows how many times during the day. And after two, three months, I think, the man came to me and said: "Mother, my wife is expecting a baby."

See? You must have the deep confidence in her. She's Mother of Jesus. She's our Mother; and she will never, never allow anything to happen to a family because she loves you, and her Son loves you tenderly. Ask her again and again to be a Mother to you.

I find this little prayer a great help, and when I need something—what do you say?—in *advance,* tell Our Lady: "Mary, Mother of Jesus, be Mother to me *now!*" (Talk 3).

SATURDAY

"Make our hearts 'meek and humble'"

Let us beg Our Lady to make our hearts "meek and humble" like her Son's was. It was from her and in her that the heart of Jesus was formed. We learn humility through accepting humiliation cheerfully. We have been created for greater things; why stoop down to things that will spoil the beauty of our hearts? How much can we learn from Our Lady! She made use of the almighty power that was in her. Tell Our Lady to tell Jesus, "They have no wine", the wine of humility and meekness, of kindness, of sweetness . . . (LC, 75–76).

FAMILY LOVE

"Therefore a man leaves his father and his mother and cleaves to his wife, and they become one flesh" (Gen 2:24).

THIRTEENTH SUNDAY
AFTER PENTECOST

They shall cleave to one another

In the Scripture we read about the family. The husband and wife, they cleave to each other, and they become one. They *cleave*. That is a very beautiful word you family people should know. Nothing, nobody, can separate us from each other. This is like Saint Paul used to say: Nothing, nobody, no persecution, no this, no that—he had a whole line—but we, we just say that one: Nothing, nobody can separate us from the love of Christ. One family. One. Undivided love for Christ. One heart in the heart of God (Talk 4).

MONDAY

Saint Joseph's love

Saint Joseph is the most wonderful example! When he realized that Mary was with child, he had only to do one thing: to go to the head, to the priest, and say, "My wife has a child, not mine." That's all he had to do and they would have stoned Mary. They would have stoned her; that was the rule. But what he did: he loved Mary so much—he didn't know anything, but it was said that she was pregnant. And then he decided, "I'll run away." And the rule was that . . . if he had run away and left his wife pregnant, they would stone him.

See the tender love of Saint Joseph for Mary? He didn't know anything; he didn't understand anything; nobody told him anything; and yet he loved her so much that he would rather the people would stone him than her. This is the love that I pray for you (Talk 3).

TUESDAY

My own mother

I'll never forget my own mother. She used to be very busy the whole day, but as soon as the evening used to come, she used to move very fast to get ready to meet my father. At that time we didn't understand; we used to smile; we used to laugh; and we used to tease her; but now I remember what a tremendous, delicate love she had for him. Didn't matter what happened, but she was ready there with a smile to meet him.

Today we have no time. The father and mother are so busy. The children come home and there's no one to love them, to smile at them (Talk 1).

WEDNESDAY

Home to the homeless Christ

. . . To offer a home to the homeless Christ, start by making our own homes places where peace, happiness and love abound, through your love for each member of your family and for your neighbors (SMT, 61).

THURSDAY

Family first

Where does . . . love propagate? It begins at home. That's why I am very strict with the Co-Workers. I always say, "Family first." That is the best meeting place. If you have to wash the napkins [diapers] for the baby, if you have to cook dinner for your husband, first that. That is the best meeting place. . . . Because if you are not there, where there is love for one another, how will your love grow for one another? (Talk 4).

FRIDAY

Helping others comes from own family

I learned how to work hard as a child. And I think that the idea of helping others came from our people, our own family. My mother was devoted to Jesus, and she taught us to pray (TW, 81).

SATURDAY

Look straight into our families

Maybe our children, our husband, our wife are not hungry, are not naked, are not homeless. But are you sure there is no one there who feels unwanted, unloved? Let us look straight into our own families. For love begins at home (TL, 8).

EMPTYING SELF

"If a man wishes to go after Me, he must deny his very self" (Mt 16:24).

FOURTEENTH SUNDAY
AFTER PENTECOST

More room for God

. . . The more we empty ourselves, the more room we give God to fill us. . . . The more you forget yourself, the more Jesus will think of you. The more you detach yourself from self, the more attached Jesus is to you (LS, 48).

MONDAY

How empty?

. . . It is not how much we really "have" to give—but how empty we are—so that we can receive fully in our life and let Him live His life in us (SV, 388).

TUESDAY

Love increases as selfishness decreases

The Spirit pours love, peace, joy into our hearts proportionately to our emptying ourselves of self-indulgence, vanity, anger and ambition, and to our willingness to shoulder the Cross of Christ (LS, 62).

WEDNESDAY

Riches can suffocate

Riches, material or spiritual, can suffocate you if they are not used in the right way. . . . Remain as "empty" as possible, so that God can fill you. Even God cannot put anything into what is already full. He does not impose Himself on us. It is you who are going to fill the world with the love God has bestowed on you (LC, 60).

THURSDAY

Am I kind and gentle?

"Love is patient. Love is kind." Because I love Jesus, am I kind? Because I love Jesus, am I gentle? Let me empty myself of all selfishness to enable God to fill me with His love (Unpub.).

FRIDAY

Unite with will of God

Separate your heart from earthly motives and unite yourself to the will of God (Unpub.).

SATURDAY

Love empties us of self

Love to be real must cost; it must hurt; it must empty us of self (Unpub.).

LOVE UNTIL IT HURTS

"And whoever would be first among you must be slave of all"
(Mk 10:44).

FIFTEENTH SUNDAY AFTER PENTECOST

Let us love until it hurts

I . . . tell my Sisters: "Let us not love in words but let us love until it hurts. It hurt Jesus to love us: He died for us. And today it is your turn and my turn to love one another as Jesus loved us. Do not be afraid to say yes to Jesus" (MLP, 37).

MONDAY

Loving the child more than themselves

In [our] leprosy centers where we are looking after all the lepers, we are building a Child's Home.

The miracle of God is that the child born of leprosy patients is at its birth perfectly clean, perfectly healthy. Before the child is born, we prepare the parents to give it up for the sake of its future. They must give it straight away before they even kiss the child, before they start feeding the child.

We take care of the child.

One day, I saw a mother and a father lay their newborn baby of three days between them. They put the baby between them and each one looked at the little one, their hands going close to the child and then withdrawing, trying, wanting to kiss the child and again falling back.

I cannot forget the deep love of that father and mother for their little child. I took the child and I could see the father and mother as I was walking. I held the child toward them and they kept on looking until I disappeared from their eyes. The agony and pain it caused!

It hurt them to give up the child, but because they loved the child more than they loved themselves, they gave it up. They are allowed to see the child, but they are not allowed to touch him.

It is beautiful to see that big sacrifice that our leper parents have to make for the sake of their children, so that the children will not be infected! (MLP, 85–86).

TUESDAY

"I love beautiful saris"

Once a very rich Hindu lady came to see me. She sat down and said, "You know, Mother, I want to share in your work." (More and more people are saying that in India now.) I said it was very wonderful. But she made a mistake and said, "You know, I love beautiful saris." (She had a most expensive sari of 800 rupees. Mine is only eight rupees; hers was 800 rupees.) And so she said, "I love beautiful and expensive saris. I go every month and buy a sari."

I prayed a little bit to Our Lady to give her the right answer how she would share in the work. And I said, "I'd better begin with the sari. You know, next time, when you go to buy a sari, instead of buying a sari of 800 rupees, you buy a sari of 500 rupees and with the remaining 300 you buy saris for the poor people."

And so, the poor thing has come down to paying 100 for a sari. I have told her, "Please do not go below 100!"

She said it had changed her life. She has really understood sharing. And she has told me that she has received much more than she has given (MLP, 78–79).

WEDNESDAY

"His suffering will not lessen mine"

We have a home for the alcoholics in Melbourne, a home for homeless alcoholics. One of them was very badly hurt by another. Then I thought this would be a case for the police. So we sent for the police and the police came and asked that gentleman, "Who did that to you?" He started telling all kinds of lies, but he wouldn't tell the truth; he wouldn't give the name, and the policeman had to go away without doing anything. Then I asked him, "Why did you not tell the police who did that to you?" He looked at me and said, "His suffering is not going to lessen my suffering."

He hid the name of his brother to save him from suffering. How beautiful and how great is the love of our people, and this is a continual miracle of love that's spread among our people. We call them poor, but they are rich in love! (MLP, 71–72).

THURSDAY

He loved until it hurt

Christ suffered. He experienced poverty. He was the object of jealousy. He was derided, ridiculed and humiliated. He knew torture and He was then crucified.

Christ also knew love, kindness, compassion and sympathy. He loved until it hurt. He understood loneliness and despair, yet He loved until it hurt.

He loved us so much—He was hurt so much through His love that He became the Bread of Life, and made himself available for us all to take—even for a little child to take.

When we take this Bread of Life we have Christ in us—we too have God's Divine Son. We too are sons of God, and we are in Christ as He is in us (L, 45).

FRIDAY

People want to see Christ

Are we helping the poor, the lonely, the oppressed?

People want to see Christ in others. Therefore, we must love Christ with undivided love until it hurts. It must be a total surrender, a total conviction that nothing separates us from the love of Christ. We belong to Christ (L, 47).

SATURDAY

Don't be afraid to show love

There is so much love in us all, but we are often too shy to express our love and we keep it bottled up inside us. We must learn to love, to love until it hurts, and we will then know how to accept love.

We must be a channel of peace.
We must love until it hurts.
We must be Christ.
We must not be afraid to show our love (L, 47).

MOTHER TERESA TALKS TO YOUTH

"Let no one despise your youth, but set the believers an example in speech and conduct, in love, in faith, in purity" (1 Tim 4:12).

SIXTEENTH SUNDAY AFTER PENTECOST

On the day you get married

I have one prayer for young people. It is very beautiful for a young man to love a young woman and for a young woman to love a young man; but make sure that on the day that you get married you have a pure heart, a virgin heart, a heart full of love; purity and virginity. Help them, help the young people by your prayers to keep their bodies and their soul pure. What we see in the streets sometimes is not love—that's passion. Let us pray, let us ask Our Lady to give us her heart so beautiful, so pure, so immaculate. Her heart so full of humility; so that we may love Jesus as she loved Him, with a pure heart, full of love and compassion. I will pray for you that you may grow in the love of God by loving one another as God loves each one of you (S, Assisi, Italy, June 6, 1982).

MONDAY

You are the future

And to all the young people I say: you are the future
for family life. You are the future of the joy of loving.
You are the future of making of your life something
beautiful for God . . . a pure love. That you love a girl
or that you love a boy is beautiful. But don't spoil it,
don't destroy it. Keep it pure. Keep your heart virgin.
Keep your love virgin, so that on the day of your marriage you can give something really beautiful to each
other . . . the joy of a pure love.

And if a mistake happens, do not destroy the child;
help each other to want the child . . . to accept the child,
the unborn child. Do not destroy it, because one mistake
should not be followed with another evil. To destroy
the unborn child is an evil. Maybe it was the mistake
of passion, but still that life is God's life, and you—the
two of you together—must protect it, must love it and
must take care of it. Because that child is created in the
image of God, is the gift of God (RL, 9).

TUESDAY

Love for Jesus in action wherever you are

. . . The work that the Church has entrusted to us is our love for Jesus in action and so your love for Jesus in action is what you do today—as young people, some of you are studying, some are working, some are preparing for the future, but all with the conviction, and that tremendous and tender love for Christ. And with Him, and through Him we will be able to do great things (CW, no. 26).

WEDNESDAY

No wedding clothes, no wedding feast

Sometime back two young people came to our house and they gave me lots, lots of money. And I said, "Where, where did you get so much money?" And they said, "Two days ago we got married, and before marriage we decided we will buy no wedding clothes, we will have no wedding feast. We will give you the money." For a Hindu family that's a big, big, big sacrifice because wedding day is one of the biggest days in their life. And again I offered, "Why, why did you do that?" And they said, "We love each other so much that we wanted to share the joy of loving with the people you serve, and we experience the joy of loving" (Talk 4).

THURSDAY

The blessing of vocations

God has blessed our Society with many vocations. We have many, many young people who have consecrated their lives to serve Christ in the poorest of the poor—to give their all to Him. And it has been a wonderful gift of God to the whole world that through this work, the rich and poor have come to know each other, to love each other and to share with the joy of loving by putting their love, their understanding love, into living action (CW, no. 26).

FRIDAY

Youth in search of selflessness

. . . The young are the builders of tomorrow. Youth today is in search of selflessness and, when it finds it, is prepared to embrace it. It is not possible to engage in the apostolate without being a soul of prayer, without consciously forgetting oneself and submitting to God's will. Our activity is truly apostolic only to the extent that we let Christ work in us and through us, with all His power, all His desire and all His love (CW, no. 24).

SATURDAY

The revolution!

One by one, since 1949, I saw young girls arriving. They had been my students. They wanted to give everything to God, and they were in a hurry to do it. They took off their expensive saris with great satisfaction in order to put on our humble cotton sari. They came fully aware that this was a very difficult thing. When a girl who belongs to a very old caste comes to place herself at the service of the outcasts, we are talking about a revolution. The biggest one. The hardest of all: the revolution of love! (AP, 103).

REVERENCE FOR LIFE

"Whoever welcomes a child welcomes Me" (Mk 9:37).

SEVENTEENTH SUNDAY
AFTER PENTECOST

Life is sacred

The life of every human being is sacred as the creation of God, and is of infinite value because He created each person including the unborn child (RL, 3).

The image of God is on that unborn child . . . (SV, 392).

MONDAY

Nations which destroy life are the poorest

For me . . . life is the most beautiful gift of God to mankind, therefore people and nations who destroy life by abortion and euthanasia are the poorest—for they have not got food for one more child, home for one old person. So they must add one more cruel murder into this world (SV, 407).

TUESDAY

An act against God's creation

The child needs love and care to fulfill God's desire of loving the world through the child. To harm the child is an act against God's creation (RL, 5).

WEDNESDAY

Nuclear bomb

The presence of the nuclear bomb in the world has created fear and distrust among nations, as it is one more weapon to destroy human life—God's beautiful presence in the world (RL, 21).

THURSDAY

Unborn child destroyed by fear

It is very painful to accept what is happening in Western countries: a child is destroyed by the fear of having too many children and having to feed it or to educate it. I think they are the poorest people in the world, who do an act like that.

A child is a gift of God.

I feel that the poorest country is the country that has to kill the unborn child to be able to have extra things and extra pleasures. They are afraid to have to feed one more child!

In Calcutta we are trying to fight abortion by adoption. In India, actually, they may leave a child in the dustbin, they may leave him in a dark door, but they would never kill the child (MLP, 61).

FRIDAY

Life belongs to God

I do not say legal or illegal, but I think that no human hand should be raised to kill life, since life is God's life in us, even in an unborn child. And I think that the cry of these children who are killed before coming into the world must be heard by God. . . .

Jesus said that we are much more important in the eyes of His Father than the grass, the birds and the flowers of the earth. And that if He takes care of these things, how much more He would take care of His own life in us. He cannot deceive us. Life is God's greatest gift to human beings, and humans are created in the image of God. Life belongs to God and we do not have the right to destroy it (LC, 40).

SATURDAY

Child God's greatest gift to family

What was the Good News that Christ had come to give? That God is love. That God loves you. God loves me. That God has made you and made me for greater things . . . to love and to be loved. We are not just a number in the world. That's why it is so wonderful to recognize the presence of that unborn child, the gift of God. The greatest gift of God to a family is the child, because it is the fruit of love.

And it is so wonderful to think that God has created a child, has created you, has created me, that very poor person in the street. That hungry person, that naked person, He has created in His image, to love and to be loved, not to be just a number.

And we read something very beautiful in the Scripture, also, where God speaks, and He says: "Even if a mother could forget her child, I will not forget you. I have carved you in the palm of My hand. You are precious to Me. I have called you by your name."

That is why as soon as a child is born, we give it a name. The name God has called from all eternity—to love and to be loved (RL, 3–5).

EFFECTS OF LOVE

" . . . Perfect love casts out fear" (1 Jn 4:18).

EIGHTEENTH SUNDAY AFTER PENTECOST

Happiness returns

At times we can actually see happiness return to the lives of the dispossessed once they realize that many of us really care about them. And if they are sick, their health improves as well (SMT, 20).

MONDAY

"I have lived like an animal . . ."

In Calcutta our Sisters and Brothers work for the poorest of the poor, who aren't wanted, aren't loved, are sick and die, for the lepers and the little children, but I can tell you I have never yet in these twenty-five years heard a poor person grumble or curse or feel miserable. I remember I picked up a person from the streets who was nearly eaten up with maggots, and he said, "I have lived

like an animal in the street, but I am going to die like
an angel, loved and cared for." And he did die like an
angel—a very beautiful death (GG, 56).

TUESDAY

"God loves me"

Some months back a man had been picked up from the
streets of Melbourne, an alcoholic, who had been for
years in that state; and the Sisters took him to their
Home of Compassion. The way they touched him, the
way they took care of him—suddenly, to him it was
clear: "God loves me."

He left the home, never touched alcohol again, went
back to his family, to his children, to his job. And after,
when he got his first salary, he came to the Sisters and
gave the money and said: "I want you to do for them,
to be the love of God to them as you have been to me."
That simple work (Talk 1).

WEDNESDAY

"Bring the priest also"

It happened, also, to an old man whom the Sisters dis-
covered in such a distressing situation. They did the
humble work for him, and then this man after two days

said to the Sisters: "You have brought God in my life. Bring the priest also." And they brought the priest. He made his confession after sixty years, and next day, he died.

It is not what we do or how much we do, but how much love we put into the action because that action is our love for God in action (Talk 1).

THURSDAY

Closer to God

. . . Every work of love, done with a full heart, always brings people closer to God (MLP, 21).

FRIDAY

"Please say that again!"

We have thousands of lepers. They are so great, they are so beautiful in their disfigurement! In Calcutta, we give them a Christmas party every year. Last Christmas I went to them and I told them that what they have is the gift of God, that God has a very special love for them, that they are very dear to Him, that what they have is not a sin.

An old man who was completely disfigured, tried to come near to me and he said, "Repeat that once more.

It did me good. I have always heard that nobody loves us. It is wonderful to know that God loves us. Please say that again!" (MLP, 83).

SATURDAY

"Sharing my pain with Jesus"

We have opened a house in New York for the AIDS and now we are going to open one in Washington. What a change in those people's lives! I can't tell you! I can't believe that it's the people who had been rejected, unwanted, unloved, the rejects. Why? Because they have received love by the Sisters. Seven of them died a beautiful death and will go straight to heaven. A complete change in their lives. Why? That love, that care, to have somebody who loves them.

. . . Thousands, thousands of AIDS-diseased young people roaming the streets. Are we there? Do we know them? Do we do something?

. . . The other day I went to hospital . . . and there one man, he said, "Mother Teresa, I want to speak to you privately." I said, "Is there something private you want to tell me?"

"I get terrible pains and I share my pain with the pain of Jesus He had in the crown of thorns." A few months ago he was a man without love, without peace of mind, who for twenty years had not been to confession—something like that. But he has found Jesus and to share.

"That day I share with the scourging, with the terrible pains Jesus had when they scourged Him. And when I get pain in my hands, I share it with the pain of Jesus when He was crucified."

And so he took every part of his body. See? He has found joy. Without even knowing, in his disease, he has found joy.

And then we brought him home and I took him to the chapel, and he bowed before the Blessed Sacrament. There was a big cross in their chapel. He was looking, looking, looking—and really, I've never seen anybody, even myself, I've never looked at the cross like that, like that man. Yet you could see the exchange of love between the two of them, between Jesus and him—really! I've never seen anything like that. I'm saying this just to give you something to think and to pray over because there is a great need of the United States today (Talk 3).

". . . AND A LITTLE CHILD SHALL LEAD THEM"

"Let the little children come to Me; do not stop them; for it is to such as these that the Kingdom of God belongs. I tell you solemnly, anyone who does not welcome the Kingdom of God like a little child will never enter it" (Mk 10:14–15).

NINETEENTH SUNDAY AFTER PENTECOST

"My mother is sick"

In our schools in Calcutta we give free bread and milk to all the children, and I noticed one day that one little girl took her bread and hid it. I asked her why she was not eating the bread and she told me: "My mother is very sick at home. We have no food in the house at all and I want to take this bread for her to eat."

That is real love, real sharing, children could learn from that (P, 58).

MONDAY

"Send my Communion dress to Mother Teresa"

There was a little girl in America who had just made her First Holy Communion. She told her parents: "I already have a white dress. Please send my Communion dress to Mother Teresa so that she can give it to a poor child." The parents of that child wrote to me and said: "It would not have occurred to us. Our little girl has taught us the joy of sharing what we have" (P, 58).

TUESDAY

Birthday wish

A little boy in a wealthy family in Calcutta was having a birthday. His parents always gave him a lot of presents and a big party. This year he asked them to give all the money they would spend on him to Mother Teresa. And on the morning of his birthday they brought him down in the car and handed me an envelope with the money in it.

That child taught his parents so much. That is love in action. Tell the children that. And tell them also that many children in Calcutta now do not invite their own friends to a birthday party. They come instead to our Children's Home and have the party there with our children as guests (P, 58).

WEDNESDAY

"I will give my sugar to Mother Teresa"

I can never forget how a little child, a Hindu child, taught me how to love the great love. In Calcutta, we didn't have sugar; and a little Hindu child, four years old, he heard Mother Teresa has no sugar. And he went home and he told his parents: "I will not eat sugar for three days. I will give my sugar to Mother Teresa." After three days, the parents brought the child to our house. In his hand he had a little bottle of sugar . . . the sugar of a little child. He could scarcely pronounce my name, but he knew he loved a great love because he loved until it hurt. It hurt him to give up sugar for three days. But that little child taught me that to be able to love a great love, it is not how much we give but how much loving is put in the giving (RL, 17).

THURSDAY

"Professor of Love"

Always I will remember the last time I visited Venezuela. A very rich family had given the Sisters land to build a Children's Home, so I went to thank them. And there in the family, I found the first child was terribly disabled. And I asked the mother, "What is the child's name?" And the mother answered me, "Professor of Love. Because this child is teaching us the whole time how to love in action." There was a beautiful, beautiful smile on the mother's face. "Professor of Love" they called their child, so terribly disabled, so disfigured; from that child they were learning how to love (RL, 17).

FRIDAY

A beautiful sacrifice

A little child was making her First Communion, and she told her parents, "I don't want you to buy anything for me. I will make my first Communion in my uniform. But you give me that money that you would spend and I will send it to Mother Teresa." Then the father said, "My child, she is doing like that—I also will give up something." So he gave up drinking. The mother said, "My child is doing like that, I will give up something, also. I'll give up smoking." So between the father and the mother and the child, the gift came. . . . They shared from so far, shared the joy of loving. It was a beautiful sacrifice. At home in the family to share the joy of loving was the child, a little child (Talk 4).

SATURDAY

Hungry all over again

Tell them about the little girl I picked up in a Calcutta street. She was about six years old and I could tell from her face that she was hungry and hadn't eaten for days. Then I gave her a crust of bread and she started to eat it, slowly, one crumb at a time. And I said, "Eat the bread, go on, eat it." And the child replied: "I am afraid, because when the bread is finished I shall be hungry all over again."

That child could teach all children something. She is their sister (P, 57).

LOVE AS SACRIFICE

"Jesus looked steadily at him and loved him, and he said, 'There is one thing you lack. Go and sell everything you own and give the money to the poor, and you will have treasure in heaven; then come, follow Me.' But his face fell at these words and he went away sad, for he was a man of great wealth" (Mk 10:21).

TWENTIETH SUNDAY AFTER PENTECOST

How did the Father love us?

. . . Jesus has asked us to love one another again and again, as the Father has loved Him. And how did the Father love Him? By asking Him to sacrifice Himself, through giving Him to die for us (MTC, 179).

MONDAY

Give what costs you

I hope you are not giving only your surplus. You must give what costs you, make a sacrifice, go without something you like, that your gift may have value before

God. Then you will be truly brothers and sisters to the poor who are deprived of even the things they need (MLP, 32).

TUESDAY

What is given you is given to share

We give the dying tender love and care—everything possible that the rich get for their money, we give [the poor] for love of God. . . . If people in the United States do not answer the needs of other people . . . they will miss the touch of Christ in their lives. What is given them is given to share, not to keep (SV, 280).

WEDNESDAY

Money is not enough

Let us not be satisfied with just giving money; money is not enough, for money one can get. The poor need our hands to serve them; they need our hearts to love them. The religion of Christ is love, the spreading of love (GG, 51).

THURSDAY

Touch and understand

I don't want you to give from your abundance. I want you to touch to understand. We are not social workers but contemplatives in the world. In our work amongst the poorest of the poor we are touching Jesus all the twenty-four hours . . . (LS, 55).

FRIDAY

Live poverty to understand it

To know the problem of poverty intellectually is not to understand it. It is not by reading, taking a walk in the slums, admiring and regretting that we come to understand it and to discover what it has of bad and good. We have to dive into it, live it, share it (LS, 55–56).

SATURDAY

Opportunities to love

We do not want people to give from their abundance. We are giving opportunity to people to love others. It is a chance given to them.

I would like more people to give their hands to serve and their hearts to love—to recognize the poor in their own homes, towns and countries and to reach out to them in love and compassion, giving where it is most needed (MLP, 33).

SPIRITUAL POVERTY

"For you say, I am rich, I have prospered, and I need nothing; not knowing that you are wretched, pitiable, poor, blind and naked" (Rev 3:17).

"Behold I stand at the door and knock . . ." (Rev 3:20).

TWENTY-FIRST SUNDAY AFTER PENTECOST

Spiritual poverty of Western world

The spiritual poverty of the Western world is much greater than the physical poverty of our people. You in the West have millions of people who suffer such terrible loneliness and emptiness. They feel unloved and unwanted.

These people are not hungry in the physical sense but they are in another way. They know they need something more than money, yet they don't know what it is. What they are missing really is a living relationship with God (LS, 13–14).

MONDAY

Greatest poverty

I find the poverty in the West much more difficult, much greater than the poverty I meet in India, in Ethiopia and in the Middle East, which is a material poverty. For example, when a few months ago, before coming to Europe and America, I picked up a woman from the streets of Calcutta, dying of hunger, I had only to give her a plate of rice and I satisfied her hunger. But the lonely and the unwanted and the homeless, the shut-ins who are spending their lives in such terrible loneliness, who are known by the number of their room and not by their name! I think this is the greatest poverty that a human being cannot bear and accept and go through (MLP, 55).

TUESDAY

Hungry for God

The poor are hungry for God; they want to hear about Our Lord. They do not worry so much about material things; they want to hear that they have a Father in heaven who loves them (MTC, 140).

WEDNESDAY

Different kinds of poverty

There are different kinds of poverty. In India some people live and die in hunger. There, even a handful of rice is precious. In the countries of the West there is no material poverty in the sense in which we speak of poverty. There no one dies of hunger; no one even is hungry in the way we know it in India and some other countries.

But in the West you have another kind of poverty, spiritual poverty. This is far worse. People do not believe in God, do not pray. People do not care for each other. You have the poverty of people who are dissatisfied with what they have, who do not know how to suffer, who give in to despair. This poverty of heart is often more difficult to relieve and to defeat. In the West you have many more broken homes, neglected children, and divorce on a huge scale (MTC, 227–228).

THURSDAY

Trying to do without God

People now are trying to prove that they can do things, that they don't need God in their lives, that they are all-powerful. And so, trying to do things without God, they are producing more and more misery and poverty (MLP, 54).

FRIDAY

We are all poor

Before God we are all poor (LC, 4).

SATURDAY

We are all handicapped

We are all handicapped in one way or another. . . . Sometimes it can be seen on the outside; sometimes it is on the inside (SV, 276).

HOLINESS

". . . But as He who called you is holy, be holy yourselves in all your conduct; since it is written, 'You shall be holy, for I am holy'" (1 Pet 1:15–16).

TWENTY-SECOND SUNDAY AFTER PENTECOST

Created to be holy

Where God is, there is love. And where there is love, there is always service. Because we, as Christians, have been created for greater things: we have been created to be holy because we have been created in the image of God (MLP, 73).

MONDAY

First step toward holiness

Holiness consists in doing God's will joyfully. Faithfulness makes saints. The spiritual life is a union with Jesus: the divine and the human giving themselves to each other. The only thing Jesus asks of us is to give ourselves to Him, in total poverty, and total self-forgetfulness.

The first step toward holiness is the will to become holy. Through a firm and upright will we love God, we choose God, we hasten to God, we reach Him, we have Him (LC, 20).

TUESDAY

Holiness not a luxury

Holiness is not the luxury of the few but a simple duty for you and me, so let us be holy as Our Father in heaven is holy. Saint Thomas says: "Sanctity consists in nothing else but a firm resolve"—the heroic act of a soul abandoning itself to God.

Our progress in holiness depends on God and on ourselves—on God's grace and on our will to be holy. We must have a real living determination to reach holiness. "I will be a saint" means I will despoil myself of all that is not God, I will strip my heart of all created things, I will live in poverty and detachment, I will renounce my will, my inclinations, my whims and fancies, and make myself a willing slave to the will of God . . . (LS, 24).

WEDNESDAY

Faithful to little things

Nothing can make us holy except the presence of God
. . . and to me the presence of God is in fidelity to little
things (Unpub.).

THURSDAY

Become holy so Christ can live in you

We must become holy, not because we want to feel
holy, but because Christ must be able to live His life
fully in us. We are to be all love, all faith, all purity, for
the sake of the poor we serve. And once we have learned
to seek God and His will, our contacts with the poor
will become the means of great sanctity to ourselves and
to others (GG, 74–75).

FRIDAY

Sanctity built on conviction of love

. . . Am I convinced of Christ's love for me and mine for Him? This conviction is like a sunlight which makes the sap of life rise and the buds of sanctity bloom. This conviction is the rock on which sanctity is built (SV, 377).

SATURDAY

I can see Jesus in you

I'm very happy if you can see Jesus in me, because I can see Jesus in you. Holiness is not just for a few people. It's for everyone, including you, sir. (To a reporter who asked her what it feels like to be called a "living saint" [SV, 382].)

My prayer is with each of you—and I pray that each one of you will be holy, and so spread His love everywhere you go. Let His light of truth be in every person's life, so that God can continue loving the world through you and me (AP, 8).

DYING

"Precious in the sight of the Lord is the death of His saints"
(Ps 116:15).
"Blessed are the dead who die in the Lord henceforth" (Rev 14:13).

TWENTY-THIRD SUNDAY AFTER PENTECOST

(or Feast of All Saints)

Eternal life is theirs

. . . We choose to celebrate this jubilee on the first of November . . . because it is for Christians the Feast of All Saints, of all those who died with the love of God and whose souls enjoy the bliss of heaven. And I believe that all our people who have died so beautifully in the Kalighat Nirmal Hriday, offering willingly their lives to God, enjoy now the happiness of the vision of God.

So we shall remember all of them on the first of November (MTC, 145–146).

MONDAY

Death is going home to God

Death is going home, yet people are afraid of what will come so they do not want to die. If we do, if there is no mystery, we will not be afraid. There is also the question of conscience—"I could have done better." Very often as we live, so we die. Death is nothing but a continuation of life, the completion of life. The surrendering of the human body. But the heart and the soul live forever. They do not die. Every religion has got eternity—another life; this life is not the end; people who believe it is, fear death. If it was properly explained that death was nothing but going home to God, then there would be no fear (HP, 140).

TUESDAY

Poor are freer to leave happy

We contemplate death every day. It is beautiful to see these people die with such dignity, radiating happiness because they are going back to where they came from, returning to the only one who loves them. Those who own many things, who own abundant goods and riches, are obsessed with them. They think that what counts the most are riches. That is why they find it hard to leave everything. This is much easier for the poor who are so free because their freedom allows them to leave happy (AP, 109).

WEDNESDAY

Something beautiful

I am very sure that all those people who have died with us are in heaven. They are really saints. They are in the presence of God.

It may be that they were not wanted on this earth but they are very beloved children of God.

I would like you to pray and to thank God for all the beautiful things our Sisters have done in the Home for the Dying.

Death is something beautiful: it means going home.

Naturally, we feel lonely for that person. But it is a very beautiful thing: a person has gone home to God (MLP, 89).

THURSDAY

Care of the dying

Our Homes for the Dying are treasure houses for the opportunities they afford us to reach souls. Death—sacred to all men—is the final stage of complete development on this earth. Having lived well, we wish for ourselves and for all men to die beautifully and so enter into the eternal life of full development in God. We train ourselves to be extremely kind and gentle in touch of hand, tone of voice and in our smile, so as to make the mercy of God very real and to induce the dying person to turn to God with filial confidence (MTC, 149).

We take great care of the dying. I am convinced that even one moment is enough to ransom an entire miserable existence, an existence perhaps believed to be useless. All souls are precious to Jesus, who paid for them with His blood (MTC, 221).

FRIDAY

Why not me?

Why these people and not me? That person picked up from the drain, why is he here, why not me? That is the mystery. Nobody can give the answer. But it is not for us to decide; only God can decide life and death. The healthy person may be closer to dying or even more dead than the person who is dying. They might be spiritually dead, only it doesn't show. Who are we to decide? (HP, 142).

SATURDAY

No slums in heaven

I remember that at the beginning of my work I had a very high fever and in that delirious fever I went before Saint Peter.

He said to me, "Go back! There are no slums in heaven!"

So I got very angry with him and I said, "Very well! Then, I will fill heaven with slum people and you will have slums then!"

When somebody dies, that person has gone home to God. That's where we all have to go (MLP, 93).

DAILY LIFE

"This is the day which the Lord has made; let us rejoice and be glad in it" (Ps 118:24).

TWENTY-FOURTH SUNDAY AFTER PENTECOST

Let us bless the Lord

"Let us bless the Lord."
"Thanks be to God."
(The way in which Mother Teresa and her Sisters greet the day, their Lord and one another each morning at 4:40 A.M.)

MONDAY

Nothing is small for God

Do you play well? Sleep well? Eat well? These are duties. Nothing is small for God (LC, 114).

TUESDAY

Dress with devotion

When we dress ourselves we should with devotion remember what each article of the religious habit means to us: the sari with its blue band is a sign of Mary's modesty; the girdle made of rope is the sign of Mary's angelic purity; sandals are a sign of our own free choice; and the crucifix is a sign of love (LC, 107).

WEDNESDAY

The prayer of our day

Holy Mass is the prayer of our day, where we offer ourselves with Christ to be broken and given to the poorest of the poor (Unpub.).

Our lives are woven with Jesus in the Eucharist, and the faith and the love that come from the Eucharist enable us to see Him in the distressing disguise of the poor, and so there is but one love of Jesus, as there is but one person in the poor—Jesus (GG, 35–36).

. . . If we truly love the poor, our first contact must be with Jesus, in the Blessed Sacrament. Then it will be easy to bring our love for Jesus to the poor (LC, 17).

Do I live the Mass during the day? (Unpub.).

THURSDAY

All the days of our lives

. . . How great is our calling. How fortunate people would think themselves if they were given a chance to give personal service to the King of this world. And here we are—we can touch, serve, love Christ all the days of our lives . . . (LC, 74).

Let us all unite at the feet of Our Lady, cause of our joy, and promise to be her joy. Pray the Rosary daily and on the streets with tender devotion to Mary. Let us fly to her for help when the work for souls is hard (Unpub.).

FRIDAY

Recreation

Recreation is a means to pray better. Relaxation sweeps away the cobwebs in the mind . . . (LC, 115).

My television is the Tabernacle (Unpub.).

SATURDAY

Offer every word to God

Offer to God every word you say, every movement you make. We must more and more fall in love with God. Let it not be said that one single woman in the whole world loves her husband better than we do Christ (LC, 84).

BEING GOD'S INSTRUMENT

"We are the clay, and Thou art our potter" (Is 64:8).

TWENTY-FIFTH SUNDAY AFTER PENTECOST

I do nothing

Christ acts in me; He acts through me; He inspires me, directs me as His instrument. I do nothing. . . . He does it all (MTC, 70).

MONDAY

God's pencil

I always say I am a little pencil in the hands of God. He does the thinking. He does the writing. He does everything—and it's really hard—sometimes it's a broken pencil. He has to sharpen it a little more.

But be a little instrument in His hands so that He can use you any time, anywhere. . . . We have only to say Yes to Him (Talk 3).

TUESDAY

Work is God's work

Let there be no pride or vanity in the work. The work is God's work, the poor are God's poor. Put yourself completely under the influence of Jesus, so that He may think His thoughts in your mind, do His work through your hands, for you will be all-powerful with Him to strengthen you (GG, 36–37).

WEDNESDAY

I need Him twenty-four hours a day

I don't think there is anyone else who needs God's help and grace more than I do. I feel so forsaken and confused at times! And I think that's exactly why God uses me: because I cannot claim any credit for what gets done. On the contrary, I need His help twenty-four hours a day. And if days were longer, I would need even more of it (SMT, 27).

THURSDAY

Discouragement, a sign of pride

If you are discouraged it is a sign of pride, because it shows you trust in your own powers . . . (LC, 114).

FRIDAY

"Give Me a free hand"

One day Saint Margaret Mary asked Jesus: "Lord, what will Thou have me do?"

"Give Me a free hand", Jesus answered.

Let Him empty and transform you and afterwards fill the chalice of your hearts to the brim, that you in turn, may give of your abundance. Seek Him. Knowledge will make you strong as death. Love Him trustfully without looking back, without fear. Believe that Jesus and Jesus alone is life. Serve Jesus, casting aside and forgetting all that troubles or worries you; make loved the love that is not loved (LC, 75).

SATURDAY

"Lord, make me an instrument . . ."

"Lord, make me an instrument of Your peace. . . ."
    Yes, an instrument. I wish to be supple, obedient, docile in Your hand (MTC, 34).

All of us are but His instruments, who do our little bit and pass by (GG, 45).

"I THIRST"

"I thirst" (Jn 19:28).

TWENTY-SIXTH SUNDAY AFTER PENTECOST

Jesus' thirst for love

"I thirst", Jesus said on the Cross. He spoke of His thirst not for water but for love (Unpub.).

MONDAY

To quench the infinite thirst

This is what we are here for: to quench the infinite thirst of Jesus for souls, for love, for kindness, for compassion (Unpub.).

TUESDAY

"Give Me to drink"

Let us remember the words of Saint Therese of Lisieux: "How shall I show my love, since love shows itself by deeds?" Well, the little child Therese will strew flowers: "I will let no tiny sacrifice pass, no look, no word. I wish to profit by the smallest actions and to do them for love. . . . I will sing always even if my roses must be gathered from amidst thorns and the longer and sharper the thorns, the sweeter shall be my song."

"Our Lord", she said, "has need of our love; He has no need of our works."

The same God who declares that He has no need to tell us if He be hungry did not disdain to beg a little water from the Samaritan woman. He was thirsty, but when He said "Give Me to drink", He, the Creator of the universe, was asking for the love of His creatures (LC, 98).

WEDNESDAY

Make loved the love that is not loved

Pray lovingly like children, with an earnest desire to love much and make loved the love that is not loved.

Let us thank God for all His love for us, in so many ways and in so many places.

Let us in return, as an act of gratitude and adoration, determine to love Him (LS, 35–36).

THURSDAY

Be always ready to love

In the Gospel we often see one word: "Come to Me all", "He that cometh to Me I will not cast out", "Suffer little children to come to Me". We must be always ready to receive, to forgive, to love and to make sure we understand what God means when He says, "I say to you, as long as you did it to one of the least of My brethren, you did it to Me" (LS, 42).

FRIDAY

Doing it to somebody

. . . A Hindu gentleman said that they and we are doing social work, and the difference between them and us is that they were doing it for something and we were doing it to somebody. This is where the respect and the love and the devotion come in, that we give it and we do it to God, to Christ, and that's why we try to do it as beautifully as possible . . . (SB, 114).

SATURDAY

"I looked for one to care for me"

. . . The first time I was here in London, we went out at night. It was a terrible, cold night and we found the people on the street. And there was an old man, well-spoken man, shivering with cold. He was in front of me. In front of him there was another old man—a negro man—with his coat open. He was protecting him from the cold.

This gentleman was saying: "Take me, take me anywhere, I am longing to sleep between two sheets." He was a well-spoken man and must have had better days. But there he was. And we looked around and we could see many. Not as many as in Calcutta, not as many, maybe, as in other places, but here there are many. If there is just one, he is Jesus, he is the one that is hungry for love, for care. And as it is written in the Scripture: "I looked for one to care for Me and I couldn't find him". How terrible it would be if Jesus had to say that to us today, after dying for us on the Cross (ML, 243).

FEAST DAYS AND OTHER SPECIAL DATES CELEBRATED AND REMEMBERED BY THE MISSIONARIES OF CHARITY

January 1:
: Solemnity of Mary the Mother of God. The day Mother Teresa began her year of waiting for permission from Rome to answer her "call within a call", 1947.

January 6:
: Mother Teresa arrived in Calcutta as a postulant from Loreto Abbey, Dublin, Ireland, 1929.

February 1:
: Decree of Praise. Missionaries of Charity recognized as Society of pontifical right, 1965.

February 2:
: The Purification of Mary. The Presentation of the Child Jesus in the Temple.

March 19:
: Feast of Saint Joseph, Husband of Mary. Sister Agnes joins Mother, 1949.

March 25:
: The Annunciation. Beginning of Missionaries of Charity Contemplative Brothers, 1978.

March 26:
: The beginning of Missionaries of Charity Brothers Active, 1963.

April 11:
: Mother Teresa and first group begin their Novitiate, 1951.

April 12:
: Final Profession of Mother Teresa as Missionary of Charity; First Profession of first group, 1953.

May 1:
: Feast of Saint Joseph, the Worker.

May 14:	Mother Teresa took Final Vows as a Sister of Loreto, 1937.
May 24:	Mother Teresa's first vows in Darjeeling, as a Sister of Loreto, 1931.
May 31:	The Visitation.
June (variable):	Sacred Heart of Jesus.
June (variable):	The Immaculate Heart of Mary.
June 25:	Beginning of Missionaries of Charity Contemplative Sisters, 1976.
June 29:	Feast of Saints Peter and Paul. Feast Day of all M.C. Professed Sisters.
July 26:	Founding of Co-Workers of Mother Teresa, 1954.
August 8:	Mother Teresa left Loreto and stayed with Little Sisters of the Poor, 1948.
August 15:	The Assumption of the Blessed Virgin Mary into heaven.
August 18:	Mother Teresa went to Patna to learn basic medicine from the Medical Missionaries.
August 22:	The Queenship of Mary. M.C. Society Feast of the Immaculate Heart of Mary. Opening of first Home for the Dying, 1952.
August 26:	Mother Teresa's birthday, 1910.
August 27:	Mother Teresa's baptism, 1910.
September 8:	The Birth of Mary.
September 10:	Inspiration Day. On her way to Darjeeling by train, Mother Teresa heard a "call within a call" to leave the Loreto convent and go to work with the poor in the slums, 1946.
September 14:	Triumph of the Cross.

October 1:	Feast Day of Saint Therese of Lisieux. Mother Teresa's feast day.
October 7:	Our Lady of the Rosary. New Congregation of the Missionaries of Charity approved and instituted in Calcutta, 1950. A day of thanksgiving in all M.C. houses throughout the world.
October 31:	Foundation Day of M.C. Priests, 1984.
November 1:	All Saints Day.
November 13:	Celebration of feast of Saint Stanislaus. Feast Day of all M.C. Novices.
November 21:	The Presentation of Mary in the Temple.
November 28:	Mother Teresa left childhood home for Rathfarnham, Dublin, home of Loreto Sisters, 1928.
December 8:	The Immaculate Conception.
December 21:	Mother Teresa went for the first time to the slum, Motighil.

Observed or celebrated, in addition, are all other major religious holy days observed by the Church throughout the year.

SOURCES

AP   González–Balado, José Luis. *Mother Teresa: Always the Poor*. Liguori, Missouri: Liguori Publications, 1980.

Const   Constitution of the Missionaries of Charity. Calcutta, 1980.

CW   *The Co-Worker Newsletter,* The Co-Workers of Mother Teresa in America. Nos. 20 (1981); 21 (1982); 23 (Winter/Spring 1983); 24 (Summer, 1983); 25 (Winter/Spring, 1984); 26 (Summer/Fall, 1984); 27 (Winter/Spring, 1985); 28 (Summer/Fall, 1985); 29 (Winter/Spring, 1986).

GG   *A Gift for God: Mother Teresa of Calcutta*. New York: Harper & Row, Publishers, 1975.

HL   Marchand, Roger. *Mother Teresa of Calcutta: Her Life and Her Work*. Liguori, Missouri: Liguori Publications, 1982.

HP   Doig, Desmond. *Mother Teresa: Her People and Her Work*. Glasgow: William Collins Sons & Co. Ltd., 1976.

IN   Spink, Kathryn. *I Need Souls Like You*. San Francisco: Harper & Row, Publishers, 1984.

IT   *I Thirst*. International Link Letter for Youth Co-Workers of Mother Teresa. Villa Elena, Onor Bres Str. Ta'xbiex, Malta. No. 4.

L   Rae, Daphne. *Love Until It Hurts*. San Francisco: Harper & Row, Publishers, 1981.

LC   Gorree, Georges and Jean Barbier, (Eds.). *The Love of Christ: Spiritual Counsels, Mother Teresa of Calcutta*. San Francisco: Harper & Row, Publishers, 1982.

LS   Spink, Kathryn, (Ed.). *Life in the Spirit*. San Francisco: Harper & Row, Publishers, 1983.

ML   Spink, Kathryn. *The Miracle of Love*. San Francisco: Harper & Row, Publishers, 1981.

MLP   González–Balado, José Luis and Janet N. Playfoot, (Eds.). *My Life for the Poor*. New York: Harper & Row, 1985.

MT   Sebba, Anne. *Mother Teresa*. London: Julia MacRae Books, 1982.

MTC   LeJoly, Edward. *Mother Teresa of Calcutta: A Biography*. San Francisco: Harper & Row, Publishers, 1983.

P   Craig, Mary. *Profiles: Mother Teresa*. London: Hamish Hamilton, 1983.

RL   Hart, Corinne, (Ed.). *Respect Life: . . . In the Words of Mother Teresa of Calcutta*. Los Angeles: Franciscan Communications, 1982.

S   Cuppari, Giacomo and Virginia (Eds.). Compilation of speeches given in Italy by Mother Teresa in 1982 and 1983.

SB   Muggeridge, Malcolm. *Something Beautiful for God.* London: William Collins Sons & Co. Ltd., 1971.

SL   Le Joly, Edward. *Servant of Love.* San Francisco: Harper & Row, Publishers, 1977.

SMT   González-Balado, José Luis. *Stories of Mother Teresa: Her Smile and Her Words.* Liguori, Missouri: Liguori Publications, 1983.

SN   Delaney, John J. (Ed.). *Saints Are Now.* New York: Doubleday, 1981, pp. 155–184 (chapter on Mother Teresa written by Eileen Egan).

SV   Egan, Eileen. *Such a Vision of the Street.* New York: Doubleday and Co., Inc., 1985.

Talk 1   Tape Recording of Mother Teresa speaking at National Presbyterian Church, Washington, D.C., 1974.

Talk 2   Tape Recording of Mother Teresa speaking at St. Mary's Cathedral, San Francisco, 1982.

Talk 3   Tape Recording of Mother Teresa speaking to Co-Workers of Mother Teresa, National Meeting, St. Paul, Minn., June 23–24, 1986.

Talk 4   Tape Recording of Mother Teresa speaking to Co-Workers of Mother Teresa, San Francisco, June 19, 1986.

Talk 5   Transcript of Mother Teresa's Nobel Peace Prize Acceptance Speech, Oslo, Norway, 1979.

TL   McPortland, Joanne. *There's Love in the Air*. Los
          Angeles: Franciscan Communications, 1981.

TW   Popson, Martha. *That We Might Have Life*. Garden
          City, N.Y.: Doubleday & Co., Inc., 1981.

Unpub.   Unpublished material from Mother Teresa. San
          Francisco: Novitiate, Missionaries of Charity.

The editor and publisher wish to express their
gratitude for the permissions granted for the re-
printing of this material.